Prophecy Without Panic
A Brief Introduction to Partial Preterism

Duncan Shennea

CDNE/Vision Publishing

Shennea, Duncan.
   Prophecy without panic: a brief introduction to partial preterism.
   Includes bibliographical references.

ISBN-13: 978-1511620895

Vision Publishing
311 East Alta Vista
Ottumwa, Iowa 52501

Table of Contents

Introduction: Why Another Book on Biblical Prophecy?

"Two men walking up a hill,
One disappears, and one's left standing still,
I wish we'd all been ready.
There's no time to change your mind;
The Son has come and you've been left behind."—from the song
"I Wish We'd All Been Ready," by Larry Norman.[1]

Will You Be Left Behind?—book title.

"[Christ] sitteth on the right hand of the Father; and He shall come again, with glory, to judge both the living and the dead; whose kingdom shall have no end. . . . And I look for the resurrection of the dead, and the life of the world to come. Amen."—from the Nicene Creed.

"I once believed that there were two types of prophecy enthusiasts—those who shared my views . . . and those who had not yet heard them convincingly presented. . . . I had not been made aware of any responsible alternatives to my own view. . . . I was aware only that some Christians were so unfortunate as to set the Rapture of the church at a time different from that in my system. It was, therefore, unsettling to me when my own studies in Scripture began to confront me with details and implications that challenged my interpretive conclusions."—from an evangelical Bible school professor.[2]

Are you truly fed up with the relentless barrage of end-times speculation? Are you tired of the constant diet of fear, apprehension, and

---

[1] "I Wish We'd All Been Ready." Words and music by Larry Norman. From the album *Only Visiting This Planet*. Solid Rock Productions, 1969.
[2] Steve Gregg, *Revelation: Four Views*. Nashville: Thomas Nelson, 1997: 1.

warnings dished out by those supposedly "in the know"? Are you deeply disappointed, not only at the continuous parade of "Rapture"-oriented predictions, but also at the seemingly limitless gullibility of otherwise devout and intelligent Christians who continue to swallow these predictions and support the ministers who make them? If so, perhaps this book is for you.

On the other hand, if you have little to no idea of what is meant by these questions, if these concepts and terms are new to you, perhaps this book is for you as well. Learning from the Bible is always enjoyable and beneficial, after all, and this is an important subject.

And if you do not fit into either of these categories, if you understand and are satisfied with "prophecy teaching" as you have heard it, if you are sure you have it figured out, if you even have a chart in the back of your Bible diagramming the coming end-time events—this book is *especially* for you. You just might need to change your mind, or at least re-consider what you believe.

Some background might be helpful, not necessarily because you need to know anything about me or my life, but because my experiences as a Christian may be similar to yours as well. At one time in my Christian life, it is good that I had solid Christian mentors and several strong Christian friends to help carry me along, since my maturity level was low, my walk of love was close to nonexistent, and my faith was probably more presumptuous than not. However, I at least had one thing going for me, or so I thought: I was absolutely certain the Rapture of the Church, the great "Catching Away" of believers, was going to take place in 1981. In the "Rapture," millions of Christians would suddenly disappear as they were caught up by God into Heaven, bodily and instantaneously, leaving non-believers behind on earth to face a period of great tribulation, and I was ready to go. I was prepared, and 1981, I believed, was the scheduled year.

My rationale for this was simple: Most of the Christians I knew believed that Jesus' apocalyptic teaching in Matthew 24 covered a seven-year "Great Tribulation" period. This seven-year period came after the great catching-away event of the Rapture of the Church (from the Latin *raptus*, a seizing or catching away), in which Christian believers would be caught up to Heaven without dying. Jesus had said, "This generation shall not pass, till all these things be fulfilled" (Matthew 24:34).[3] A biblical generation was roughly forty years, and the "generation" I thought Jesus was pointing toward was the generation seeing Israel's re-establishment as a nation. (My reasons for

---

[3] All biblical references in this book will be from the King James Version of the Bible unless otherwise indicated.

thinking this are too difficult, and in retrospect too trivial, to go into at this point.)

Israel had been re-established as a nation in 1948; forty years added onto that brought us to 1988. In order for "all these things" to be fulfilled, the Great Tribulation had to be finished by that time. Therefore, seven years of Tribulation subtracted from 1988 took us back to 1981, the year of the Rapture, and *Q.E.D.*: Thus it is demonstrated. The year of the Rapture was 1981. My Christian friends agreed. The great "catching away" obviously had to happen according to our schedule.

Only it didn't happen. Perhaps we had miscalculated. At least we thought so when two books came out by previously unknown writer Edgar Whisenant, books that sold close to five million copies: *On Borrowed Time* and especially *88 Reasons Why the Rapture Could Be in 1988.* Whisenant was quite confident about the 1988 date, and specified even further that the Rapture would take place between September 11 and September 13 of that year (the time of the Jewish holiday Rosh Hoshanah). "Only if the Bible is in error am I wrong," he proclaimed, "and I say that to every preacher in town." During one interview he said, "If there were a king in this country and I could gamble with my life, I would stake my life on Rosh Hoshanah 1988" as the time for the Rapture to take place.[4] Likewise, prophecy teacher Hal Lindsey, whose 1970 work *The Late Great Planet Earth* had been a phenomenal best seller, a decade later released *The 1980s: Countdown to Armageddon.* That book declared on its cover, "The decade of the 1980s could very well be the last decade of history as we know it."[5]

Only, again, it didn't happen.

Then we decided that the year 2000 or "Y2K" was the year of Christ's returning. Again, there was a biblical reason: According to Genesis 1, there were six days of creation and then one day of rest. There had been four thousand years of human history from Adam to Christ (we believed), and two thousand from Christ to Y2K, more or less, although a slightly mistaken sixth-century calendar conversion made our numbering rather inexact. This six thousand years of human history corresponded to the six days of creation, and now it was time for the "day of rest," the thousand-year Millennial reign of Christ's established kingdom upon earth. After all, as we often quoted, didn't the Bible say that a thousand years of human history was as a day with the Lord? Also, the so-called "Y2K Bug" was supposed to crash computer systems worldwide, leading to devastation and

---

[4] Taken from "Field Guide to the Wild World of Religion." Isitso.org
[5] Hal Lindsey, *The 1980s: Countdown to Armageddon.* New York: Bantam Books, 1980: frontispiece and cover.

panic throughout the world's population. At that point the earth would experience its greatest revival, as it would be prepared for our Christian witness by its traumatic experiences.

It might be difficult at this remove to remember the anxiety and speculation of the days leading up to the year A.D. 2000. I recall one minister saying in a nation-wide broadcast, "How close is the Rapture? Well, I'll tell you one thing—don't buy any green bananas." Many people stockpiled food and water and purchased generators for the emergency supplies thought to be required. Likewise it might be difficult to remember the combined relief and disappointment when again nothing happened. A few years later (in the year 2005) I heard a minister on television arguing that the Y2K calculations were essentially correct and that God in his mercy is only granting "a sliver of time" before the Rapture takes place. Other ministers are equally sure of the shortness of time remaining in human history; as one writes:

> As we approach the Seventh Millennium [this was published in 1997], time seems to have accelerated and prophetic events are being compressed together. We have entered the triangle of the end [that is, if human history were shaped like a triangle, we would now be entering the narrow point at the apex], in which both the time allotted and prophetic events are being compressed to maximum density to fulfill all the prophetic Scriptures, and end the age in God's own time frame. . . . We are spiraling faster and faster through the narrow end of the triangle of time, for the purpose of being released into a new Millennium that will forever change planet earth.[6]

Later in the same work, the author says, "Get prepared for the most traumatic change that will ever come to this planet in six thousand years. There is no doubt about it. We are in the end-time harvest. It is the season of His appearing."[7]

But it did not happen.

One would think that eventually prophecy enthusiasts would become a bit wary in their proclamations; however, to the true enthusiast, the "correct" deadline for the Lord's return is always just ahead. For example, in the spring of 2011, radio minister Harold Camping predicted the Lord's return, the Rapture, and final judgment were due on May 21. Camping's ministry received millions of dollars in donations, but his prediction did not

---

[6] Charles Capps, *End-Time Events: Journey to the End of the Age.* Tulsa: Harrison House, 1997: 20.
[7] Ibid., p. 246.

pan out. After the date passed uneventfully, Camping revised the prediction to October 21, 2011. Some of Camping's followers were so committed to his teaching, one of them even shot a co-worker in the shoulder for teasing him about his "Rapture" expectations after the May 21 date.[8] December 21, 2012, also came and went, despite the predictions of the "Mayan Calendar" end of the world; at least we cannot blame Christians for that one. The most current prediction of which I am aware now says the Rapture will occur around September of 2015, because of the so-called "blood moons," a set of lunar eclipses supposedly having prophetic significance. (I am writing these words in 2014.)

So we've had the dates 1981, 1988, 2000, 2011, 2012, and 2015 given for the Lord's return and/or the end of the world as we know it—and that's only within my personal memory! When we look further back in Christian history, we find Christian apocalyptics who expected the end of the world in the year A.D. 1000; Joachim of Fiore, who thought the world was about to end in the twelfth century; Christopher Columbus, who in part desired to expand the reach of Christianity because of his belief the world would end in the 1500s; Martin Luther and other reformers, who believed the Protestant Reformation was an end-time fulfillment of prophecies in the book of Revelation, with the papacy in the role of the Antichrist; various groups and popular movements (such as the "Millerites") who looked for and specifically predicted Christ's return in the 1830s, the 1840s, the 1960s, and the 1970s; and the list could go on and on. By now, even people who know virtually nothing regarding biblical teaching know the phrase "Left Behind," from the immensely popular series of novels and movies about Rapture-oriented events.

So why another book on biblical prophecy? Why "Prophecy Without Panic"? If bookstores, theaters, popular culture, and Christian homes have already been flooded with such a wide variety of prophecy-related materials, what need is there for more end-times chatter amidst the chaos?

The answer is two-fold, but simple: First, I believe today's Church, as well as today's society in general, needs a revival of *accurate teaching* regarding the prophetic teachings of the Bible. Specifically, if Christianity is not to be made a laughingstock over and over again, the virus of "Rapturism" needs to be purged from our prophetic interpretations; we need to be taught, over and over again, what the Bible actually is saying in its prophetic scriptures. We need to understand the prophecies of God's Word faithfully and

---

[8] "Rapture teasing fueled shooter, victim's mom says." Associated Press, May 2011.

soberly, dismissing the hype, anxiety, and panic-mongering of most "Last Days" teaching currently out there.

The second reason is a bit less controversial in nature and perhaps a bit more "spiritual." Understanding the prophetic scriptures as they are intended to be understood has been of immense benefit in my personal spiritual life and Christian walk. Upon reading the Bible, I am continually struck at how so many seemingly perplexing passages make so much more sense, given the understanding of "Prophecy Without Panic." It is deeply reassuring and strengthening to one's faith to see both the meaning and the manifestation of the prophecies of Jesus and other New Testament authors, and to see further how these prophecies dovetail with the ancient Hebrew prophets when their words are given due balance in context and reference.

Others are also writing on these topics and explaining the prophetic Word clearly.[9] This book, *Prophecy Without Panic*, may be best considered as another voice added to the growing chorus. If it be God's will, may this chorus of voices become the common understanding of the Body of Christ as a whole; may the true importance of the prophetic scriptures begin to shine forth as light in darkness; may we think on God's prophetic scriptures with understanding and not with panic.

---

[9] For popular examples, see R.C. Sproul's *The Last Days According to Jesus* (Baker, 1998) and Hank Hanegraaff's *The Apocalypse Code* (Thomas Nelson, 2007).

1. What Is the Purpose of Biblical Prophecy?

"Encourage the apprehensive."—1 Thessalonians 5:14, *Jerusalem Bible*
"Comfort one another with these words."—1 Thessalonians 4:18

What is the purpose of biblical prophecy? Doesn't it seem odd, and perhaps a little troubling, that many of the people who are the most interested in biblical prophecy often do not seem to know its real purpose? If they are asked directly, answers are given such as the following: "The purpose of prophecy is to reveal the end times." "The purpose of prophecy is to prepare us for the Rapture, so that we can escape the Great Tribulation." "The purpose of prophecy is to help us understand current events and how they fit into God's end-time plan." "The purpose of prophecy is to give us special insight into happenings in the Middle East." And so on. In my own conversations on the subject with many well-meaning Christians through many years, I have never had anyone give me this answer: "The purpose of prophecy is to glorify the Lord Jesus Christ and help us know Him better." Yet there it is in the opening verse of the Book of Revelation, probably the best known of all prophetic books in the Bible: "The Revelation of Jesus Christ, which God gave unto him."

In other words, if one were to ask what it is that the Book of Revelation is "revealing," the answer would be something like this: First and foremost, the "revelation" of the Book of Revelation is the revelation or unveiling of Jesus Himself. We see Him as Savior, Redeemer, Teacher, Healer, and so on, in other portions of the New Testament, but in this final book we see Him as King, as Lord of all nations, indeed, of all creation, and as the coming Judge of the earth and all its inhabitants. No wonder John, the author, writes, "And when I saw him, I fell at his feet as dead" (1:17). Later in the same book, John falls again, this time before an angel of God, and the angel tells him this:

> No! Don't! For I am a servant of God just as you are, and as your brother Christians are, who testify of their faith in Jesus. Worship God. *The purpose of all prophecy and of all I have shown you is to tell about Jesus.*[10]

What a plain, straightforward statement: Prophecy should not lead us to panic or fear or apprehension, but rather directly to the worship of God, because *the purpose of all prophecy is to tell about Jesus.*

The apostle Paul makes similar points in his first epistle to the Thessalonian church; he tells us to "encourage the apprehensive" and, when speaking specifically of prophetic events, to "comfort one another with these words."[11] Yet it seems that much of what passes for teaching on biblical prophecy today actually does the opposite—that is, it actually increases apprehension and frightens instead of comforts. It definitely does not seem to reassure the nervous, but rather the reverse. I remember being more or less terrified as a teenager by the "Rapture" movies shown in our church and the corresponding preaching done from the church pulpit. Were my "robes clean"? Was I "ready"? Or would I be "left behind" to face the Antichrist's busy guillotine, as one movie vividly portrayed?

In our own day, fascination with Rapture-oriented prophecy teaching is evidenced by the sales of the fictional *Left Behind* series, co-authored by minister Tim LaHaye and writer Jerry B. Jenkins. Three movies have been made based on the series, and a big-budget remake of the first installment (starring Nicholas Cage) was recently released. These movies appear to have done well financially, although to say they received mixed reviews would be overly charitable. As of this writing, the series has sold well over 70 million books. Roughly one out of every eight Americans has read at least one of the novels in the twelve-volume series. Somewhat surprisingly, according to research done by Tyndale, the novels' publisher, "More Jews, agnostics, and atheists read the series than mainline Protestants":

> And why are so many people eager to do that? Well, check the news tonight. As the world gets increasingly scary, with much of the trouble centered in the Mideast—just where you'd expect from reading the Book of Revelation—even secular Americans sometimes wonder (or at least wonder if they ought to start wondering) whether there might not be something to this End Times stuff. . . . And it's no coincidence that the books are a favorite with American soldiers in Iraq.[12]

On the other hand, to be fair, this accusation of "fear-mongering" is perhaps not a pertinent objection to Rapture-oriented prophecy teaching *if* the teaching itself is true and accurate. If such be the case, whether or not prophecy teaching promotes comfort and peace, or promotes apprehension

---

[10] Revelation 19:10, *The Living Bible.* Emphasis added.

[11] 1 Thessalonians 5:14, *The Jerusalem Bible,* and 4:18, KJV.

[12] David Gates, "The Pop Prophets." *Newsweek* 24 May 2004: 46-47.

and fear, is beside the point. If it is true and biblical, then it should be taught, no matter what the consequences. However, one of the main points for which I plan to argue throughout this book is that much of contemporary teaching on biblical prophecy is neither true, nor accurate, nor even biblical.

This book, *Prophecy Without Panic*, briefly introduces an interpretation of biblical prophecy, the partial preterist interpretation, which I find much more satisfying and much more faithful to the overall scope of New Testament prophecy. Furthermore, this interpretative stance is also much more helpful in understanding specific prophetic verses and passages. Because this book is brief and many different topics are addressed, the following chapters also will be brief and designed to answer one or two simple questions on specific topics given in the titles for each chapter.

In that spirit, therefore, here is the quick summary conclusion for this opening chapter: What is the purpose of biblical prophecy? To answer this question, we need to remember the words of the angel to the Apostle John[13]: *The purpose of all prophecy and of all I have shown you is to tell about Jesus.* Ultimately, the purpose of biblical prophecy is to glorify the Lord Jesus Christ and help us know Him better—as Lord, as King, as the Judge of all nations and all people, as the One who holds all of us in His hands. I believe we are greatly helped to know Jesus in this way by the habit of viewing prophecy "without panic," and I hope I can convince you to think this way as well.

---

[13] Throughout this book, John the Apostle will be taken as the author of Revelation. The author of Revelation only identifies himself as John, never as an apostle or even as one who knew Jesus personally, and so it actually does not matter if the author is the apostle or someone else named John. However, the weight of tradition leans toward accepting the author as John the Apostle.

2. What Is "Prophecy Without Panic"?

"Blessed is he that readeth, and they that hear the words of this prophecy, and keep those things which are written therein: for the time is at hand."—Revelation 1:3

The Christians I know personally, especially the ones with whom I have grown throughout many years, are the best, kindest, wisest, and strongest people I know. Nothing could be further from my intention than to mock or belittle them in any way. Their dedication to our Lord, theirs and mine, is indisputable and worthy of emulation; so also is their dedication to our Lord's teachings and to the Bible as a whole. However, there is one highly interesting question I never once heard anyone ask during those years of Christian growth, years of intense Bible study and church attendance, years of worship, thought, and fellowship. The question is so simple that today I shake my head at it. Why didn't we ever think of it? Why didn't it ever come up? The question is simply this: *What did the early Christians—the very first ones who read and heard the Book of Revelation—think of it?* What did they think it meant? How did they interpret it? When they heard the statement, "The time is at hand" (Rev. 1:3), did they mentally translate that as "The time is far, far in the distant future"? If not, how *did* they translate it?[14]

The closest answer to this I ever heard from contemporary expositors of Revelation (and this I heard in more than one sermon) was simply that, if our interpretations of the book were correct, the early Christians could not possibly have known what it actually meant. The meaning of the book was "sealed up" for our generation, the generation which would see the fulfillment of all its prophecies. Only *we* could truly understand Revelation, we who were seeing before our own eyes its strange predictions coming to

---

[14] "I will assume that the book was intended to be meaningful for its first readers, who lived nearly 2,000 years ago. And that's significant, because the popular theories that assume the Revelation is describing terrorist plots in the modern world usually don't bother asking how the earliest readers would have understood the book."—Craig R. Koester, *The Apocalypse: Controversies and Meaning in Western History*. Chantilly, Virginia: The Teaching Company, 2011: 16-17.

pass. But even as those statements were made, the obvious corollary to this (obvious now, I should say) did not seem to arise in our minds: If our interpretations of biblical prophecy were correct, that meant that, through all the centuries of Christians before us, the New Testament prophecies were worse than confusing; they were literally incomprehensible. All those centuries of Christians were living in darkness as far as the plan and purpose of God was concerned, at least in the area of biblical prophecy. Everything they thought the New Testament prophecies were about *had to be mistaken*—if we were right.

Yes—if we were right.

Frankly, the Rapture-oriented prophecy teaching to which we held was the only type of prophecy teaching I had ever heard. I did not know, and I do not think the other congregation members around me knew, that there was any other possible interpretation of New Testament prophecy than that involving the Rapture (the bodily catching away of the true Church to Heaven); the seven-year "Tribulation" that was to follow, in which the Antichrist would rule (those holding this view are called "Pre-Tribulationists" or sometimes "Pre-Tribs" for short); the great Battle of Armageddon that was to follow the Tribulation; and the literal Millennium, the thousand-year reign of Christ on earth after Armageddon. We took seriously signs of the coming Tribulation; we considered carefully various nominees for the position of Antichrist. I recall the mini-flurry surrounding President Reagan for a brief moment: His name, after all, was Ronald Wilson Reagan (count the number of letters in each name). And he claimed to be a Christian! But, confusingly enough, many of us voted for him— twice. Perhaps he was not the Antichrist after all; perhaps it was Saddam Hussein. Wait—no—he died. At least the focus on the "Pre-Tribulation Rapture" kept us alert as to our own spiritual conditions. Like the young women in Jesus' parable, we wanted to be ready when the Bridegroom arrived. We listened to newscasts grimly. Everything revolved, and still revolves, around events occurring in the always tense and tumultuous Middle East. And note well: It does not matter in what year you may read these words; for the Pre-Tribulationist, the previous sentence will always remain true. Every fluctuation in the ever-shifting panorama of Middle Eastern politics causes new ripples of apprehensive prophetic speculation amongst some Christian groups, most notably Christian televangelists.

However, despite their contemporary applications, the specific teachings on the Pre-Tribulation Rapture as presented in today's church actually began in the 1820s with Edward Irving, a Scottish clergyman whom even supporters referred to as "rather unstable" and "eccentric," but "spiritually

15

sensitive."[15] These teachings then were promoted beginning in the years 1827-1830 by John Nelson Darby, a British minister of the Plymouth Brethren. In 1859 Darby also began teaching in the United States, in particular presenting his system of "dispensationalism":

> Darby taught that God has dealt with mankind in a series of epochs, or dispensations. . . . One cycle of prophesied events ended with Jesus' crucifixion; the next will begin with the *Rapture*—the moment when all believers will rise to meet Christ in the air. Once the prophetic clock begins ticking again with the Rapture, the final sequence of events will unfold with dismaying rapidity for those left behind, beginning with the seven-year reign of Antichrist and the Apostate Church, the so-called *Tribulation* (Matt. 24:21), of which the second half will be sheer hell. . . . The Tribulation will end with the *Battle of Armageddon*, when Christ, the saints, and the heavenly host return to earth and defeat Antichrist and his army. Next will come the *Millennium*, Christ's thousand-year rule on earth; a final, doomed uprising by Satan; the resurrection of the dead; and history's final event, the Last Judgment.[16]

This has become by far the best-known and most popular system of prophecy interpretation in the United States today. After Darby's ministry, dispensationalism received widespread currency by the 1909 publication of C.I. Scofield's *Scofield Reference Bible*, with Scofield's own extensive annotations and footnotes. "The line of continuity from Darby can be traced through W.E. Blackstone, G. Campbell Morgan, H.A. Ironside, A.C. Gaebelein, and C.I. Scofield to more recent times," writes professor of history Robert G. Clouse, editor of *The Meaning of the Millennium.* "Dispensationalism has become the standard interpretation for over 200 Bible institutes and seminaries in the United States. Many famous interdenominational evangelists including D.L. Moody and Billy Graham have also adopted this understanding of eschatology [the study of end-time events]."[17] Students of this system typically maintain that the symbolic images of Matthew 24, the Book of Daniel, and the Book of Revelation are

---

[15] Herbert VanderLugt, *Perhaps Today! The Rapture of the Church.* Grand Rapids, Michigan: Radio Bible Class, 1984: 85-86.

[16] Paul Boyer, *When Time Shall Be No More: Prophecy Belief in Modern American Culture.* Cambridge: Belknap Press of Harvard University Press, 1992: 87-88. Emphasis in original.

[17] Robert G. Clouse, "Foreword." In Steve Gregg, *Revelation: Four Views.* Nashville: Thomas Nelson, 1997: xiv.

closely related to each other and often linked to current events in world history.

Occasionally pre-tribulationists try to show Rapture teaching as existing in previous centuries of the Church age (before the 1800s), but for the most part lack evidence of this; for example, a single sentence from an Orthodox sermon by "Pseudo-Ephraem," probably dating from around A.D. 700, is sometimes cited.[18] Pre-tribulationist Herbert VanderLugt argues in response to this problematic lack of early evidence that "the early church fathers and their successors did not establish a systematic doctrine of last things":

> The writings of the early church fathers have been quoted by both pretribulationists and posttribulationists as supporting their position. After reading a large number of these quotations, I am convinced that these early church fathers did not teach pre-tribulationism as we understand it. But neither did they set forth a distinctive posttribulation view. . . . They have little bearing on the issues that divide Bible scholars on this controversial doctrine.[19]

"Many of us thought that the coming and going of Y2K and the beginning of a new millennium would cause people to question dispensational assumptions and preoccupations with signs of the end," writes pastor and teacher Kim Riddlebarger. He goes on: "However, the success of the *Left Behind* series of end-time novels . . . proves the influence and staying power of dispensational teaching."[20]

Despite dispensationalism's popularity, however (especially in America), the question increasingly is arising: Is dispensationalism the only honest interpretive stance a believing Christian can hold regarding the end-time scriptures? Are the doctrines of the Rapture, Great Tribulation, Antichrist, Second Coming, Millennial Reign of Christ, and Final Judgment (sometimes called the "Great White Throne" judgment, from Revelation 20:11) so immediately apparent from our reading of the Scriptures that one must accept them all or else be regarded as unfaithful to God's Word?

If one answers these questions "Yes," then, as we've already discussed, one must also regard most of the historical Christian Church as blinded with respect to the "immediately apparent" interpretation of biblical prophecy. The Church has always held to its belief in Christ's judgment of

---

[18] For an example of this citation, see Thomas Ice, "The Myth of the Origin of Pretribulationism." pre-trib.org.

[19] *Perhaps Today!* 85, 87.

[20] Kim Riddlebarger, *A Case for Amillennialism: Understanding the End Times.* Grand Rapids, Michigan, and Leicester, England: Baker Books and Inter-Varsity Press, 2003: 10.

the righteous and unrighteous, the resurrection of the dead, and life everlasting with God in eternity. But the teaching of the Rapture of the Church is notably absent from the Church's historical consensus. In early post-New Testament literature such as the Didache, the Epistles of Barnabas and Clement, Justin Martyr's "Dialogue With Trypho," and the "Vision" of the Shepherd of Hermas, Christians are described as eagerly awaiting the Lord's return, "looking for that blessed hope, and the glorious appearing of the great God and our Savior Jesus Christ" (Titus 2:13)—but awaiting this blessed hope as a Second Coming, *after* they have passed through their time of tribulation, not as a special Rapture to rescue them *from* their tribulation. As one writer says:

> The hope of the Church throughout the early centuries was the second coming of Christ, not a pretribulation rapture. If the Blessed Hope is in fact a pretribulation rapture, then the Church has never known that hope through most of its history, for the idea of a pretribulation rapture did not appear in prophetic interpretation until the nineteenth century. . . . To deduce from [the Church's] attitude of expectancy a belief in a pretribulation rapture and an any-moment coming of Christ, as has often been done, is not sound.[21]

However, there are other interpretive options available besides the "pretribulation rapture" view. Notably, there is the preterist option referred to earlier, what I have called "Prophecy Without Panic."

The preterist view will be discussed extensively in later chapters, but for now what does this phrase "Prophecy Without Panic" mean? What I mean by it may be summarized in the questions opening this chapter: What did the early Christians—the very first ones who read and heard the Book of Revelation—think of it? What did they think it meant? How did they interpret it? Once we have answered these questions, we will be able to couple our answers with the principle already established in Chapter 1 of this book: The purpose of New Testament prophecy is to tell about Jesus, that we may glorify Him better and know Him more. What did the earliest Christians think that Jesus was doing in the prophecies they were hearing and reading—such as in the Book of Revelation, for instance? How was Jesus being revealed and glorified through the prophecies to which they were listening?

---

[21] George Eldon Ladd, "The Historic Hope of the Church." From *The Blessed Hope*. Grand Rapids, Michigan: Eerdman's, 1980. Groups.msn.com/ChristianEndTimeViews.

Noted biblical scholar J. Stuart Russell speaks of these first-century Christians and their relationship to prophecy interpretation in this way:

> They lived expecting a consummation which was to arrive in their own time, and which they might witness with their own eyes. This fact lies on the very face of the New Testament writings; it is the key to the interpretation of much that would otherwise be obscure and unintelligible, and we shall see . . . how consistently this view is supported by the whole tenor of the New Testament Scriptures.[22]

It seems, then, that when first-century Christians read prophecies such as the Book of Revelation, they thought of them as having immediate and contemporary relevance to the issues, events, and historical personalities they were facing in their own lives. Should we be quick to dismiss their interpretations as mistaken? Should we assume their lack of understanding of these prophecies, prophecies which after all are many centuries closer in time to those Christians than to us?

As we begin to understand biblical prophecy with these guiding thoughts in mind, prophetic scriptures will become not only more and more illuminating, but also more and more comforting. We will see Jesus in new ways; we will understand His Word better and better. We will find ourselves looking forward to the future with new hope, in fact, and not with apprehension. We will be able to discuss biblical prophecy with accuracy and confidence, and especially without panic.

---

[22] J. Stuart Russell, *The Parousia: The New Testament Doctrine of Our Lord's Second Coming.* Grand Rapids, Michigan: Baker Books. Reprinted 1999: 26.

3. What Are the Four Main Types of Interpretation of Biblical Prophecy?

"I once believed that there were two types of prophecy enthusiasts—those who shared my views . . . and those who had not yet heard them convincingly presented. . . . I had not been made aware of any responsible alternatives to my own view. . . . I was aware only that some Christians were so unfortunate as to set the Rapture of the church at a time different from that in my system. It was, therefore, unsettling to me when my own studies in Scripture began to confront me with details and implications that challenged my interpretive conclusions."—from an evangelical Bible school professor.[23]

In the previous chapter, it was stated that the Rapture-oriented prophecy teaching which I once held was frankly the only type of prophecy teaching I had ever heard. I did not know, and I do not think the other congregation members around me knew, that there was any other possible interpretation of New Testament prophecy than that which we had always been told.

In fact, however, there are at least four basic views of biblical prophecy that have been held and promulgated by various Christians as being both scriptural and validated in history. These four views, the Futurist (which we have already been considering under the label of "Pre-Tribulation Rapture-Oriented" teaching, but will henceforth refer to as "Futurist"), the Historicist, the Symbolist, and the Preterist, all still have able defenders even today. All of them also have had well-known and devout defenders throughout Christian history. Therefore, an examination of these four views could help to demonstrate that equally faithful Christians have scriptural warrant for holding different views on the end-times teaching of the Bible.

In other words, the complex of Rapture-oriented dispensationalist teachings referred to collectively as the "Futurist" position, despite its popularity and the fact of its being the best known eschatological stance in

---

[23] Steve Gregg, *Revelation: Four Views.* 1.

America, is not necessarily the only or the best interpretive stance one might adopt. In the meantime, as we consider these thoughts, readers might also consider this question in order to determine how much of a commitment to a specific stance they may have: If a minister holds a different interpretation of biblical prophecy than you do, would you trust what that minister has to say on any other topic? For many Christians, the answer might very well be "no." But isn't that a bit of an over-emphasis?

Prophecy teaching and prophecy seminars are quite popular among a very large segment of contemporary Christianity. People are fascinated by the heightened oracular power of the prophetic scriptures and the sense of special insight or "behind-the-scenes" information that is unveiled. But because of this special power and insight, and because many prophecy teachers believe their message to be of paramount importance in our day, the in-fighting between those of differing views may wax especially bitter. For example, when Tyndale House, the publisher of Tim LaHaye's *Left Behind* novels, also published Hank Hanegraaff's *The Last Disciple* (a fictional interpretation of the book of Revelation from the Preterist point of view), LaHaye became openly angry. "They are going to take the money we made for them and promote this nonsense," LaHaye said about Tyndale's release of the book by Hanegraaff, who is best known as host of the "Bible Answer Man" radio program. "I feel the whole evangelical community has been betrayed by a major publisher that, for forty years, has been a stalwart of biblical interpretation based on a literal interpretation of the scriptures; and now they're advancing a book that destroys literalism in favor of an allegorical interpretation of history. I don't know what science fiction he [Hanegraaff] is reading." In response to the "science fiction" remark, LaHaye's own novels were described as "futuristic" and "speculative" by Sigmund Brouwer, Hanegraaff's co-author of *The Last Disciple*.[24] In contemporary Christianity, the intensity of arguments over the future seems to be rivaled only by that of arguments over the pre-historic past.

In fact, despite the dense imagery and allusive character of most biblical prophetic texts, many Christian teachers seem to regard their own interpretations as more or less self-evident and other interpretations as fanciful and speculative. "I once believed that there were two types of prophecy enthusiasts—those who shared my views . . . and those who had not yet heard them convincingly presented," writes evangelical Bible school professor Steve Gregg:

---

[24] John Draper, "*Left Behind* Co-Author Slams Contrary New Series." christian-retailing.com.

I had not been made aware of any responsible alternatives to my own view (out of charity to my teachers, I will assume that they were likewise unaware). I was aware only that some Christians were so unfortunate as to set the Rapture of the church at a time different from that in my system. It was, therefore, unsettling to me when my own studies in Scripture began to confront me with details and implications that challenged my interpretive conclusions. . . . I became aware of radically different approaches to [biblical prophecy] that made at least as much sense as did mine. Some of these views had been around much longer than mine.[25]

The view originally held by Gregg was a form of Futurist dispensationalism. Note well that he does not describe dispensationalism as unbiblical, nor as not making sense. Nor does he say that he abandoned the Futurist position. All he says is that other views "made at least as much sense." For a student and teacher of biblical prophecy, this is a major concession indeed.

So what are these "radically different approaches" to New Testament prophecy? In addition to the Futurist view, three others have already been mentioned. Here follows a brief definition and history of all four:

- **Futurist:** Futurists believe that almost all New Testament prophecy (for example, chapters 4 through 22 of the Book of Revelation) is still to be fulfilled in the future—hence the name "Futurist." Futurists typically believe in a future catching away of Christian believers (the Rapture of the Church), in which Jesus returns "in the clouds" but technically not "to the earth"; a revived European Roman Empire ruled over by a literal person who will be the Antichrist; and a seven-year Great Tribulation over the earth. At the conclusion of the seven years, Jesus will return again with the previously raptured believers and destroy his enemies in the climactic Battle of Armageddon; this is the "Second Coming," in which Jesus actually returns "to" the earth. (Sometimes the Rapture and this event are referred to as the first and second "stages" of the Second Coming.) The Second Coming will usher in a thousand-year reign of peace called the Millennium. At the end of the Millennium, Satan will be released from confinement to tempt humanity once more; following this comes the Resurrection of the Dead and their Final Judgment. Satan will be bound and punished eternally, the heavens and earth will be literally re-created, and humans will be divided into

---

[25] Steve Gregg, *Revelation: Four Views*, 1.

those spending eternity with God and those going to Hell. To reiterate: Since they believe that these are the events primarily described by New Testament prophecy, Futurists also believe almost all New Testament prophecy is as yet unfulfilled. This is probably the most popular interpretation of biblical prophecy in America today, especially among evangelical and Pentecostal Protestants.

- **Historicist:** Historicists believe that New Testament prophecy is in the process of being fulfilled throughout history, with some already behind us and some yet to occur. This was the most popular method of interpreting prophecy in Protestant Christianity from the time of the Reformation (the 1500s) until the mid-1800s. For example, Martin Luther saw the Book of Revelation as an ongoing picture of Christian and world history, with the Pope as the Antichrist and the Roman Catholic Church as the Harlot of Babylon, destined (according to Revelation 17) to be overthrown. Some Historicists believe a partial fulfillment of this prophecy took place during and immediately after the French Revolution, as the Roman Catholic Church in Europe lost much of its prestige and power. While some elements of prophecy are yet to be fulfilled in the future, Historicists typically do not believe in a future Rapture of the Church. Although the Historicist view is the least popular today, notable Christians who have held it in one form or another include Luther, John Wycliffe, John Knox, Ulrich Zwingli, John Calvin, Isaac Newton, Jonathan Edwards, Charles Finney, Matthew Henry, Adam Clarke, and Charles Spurgeon.[26]

- **Symbolist:** Typically the Symbolist does not relate New Testament prophecy to any specific time frame at all. This approach "does not attempt to find individual fulfillments of the visions but takes [New Testament prophecy] to be a great drama depicting transcendent spiritual realities, such as the spiritual conflict between Christ and Satan, between the saints and the antichristian world powers, and depicting the heavenly vindication and final victory of Christ and his saints. . . . [P]rophecy is thus rendered applicable to Christians in any age."[27] Every day and always, in other words, Christians must face tribulation and

---

[26] *Revelation: Four Views*, 34.

[27] Ibid., 2-3.

23

the Antichrist world system, but biblical prophecy gives us ongoing encouragement and reveals our ultimate victory in Christ the King—it is spiritually *representative* rather than historically *predictive*. Theologian J.A.T. Robinson provides an example of this approach; he "interprets Christ's parousia not as a literal event of the future but as a symbolical . . . presentation of what happens whenever Christ comes in love and power. . . . Judgment day is a dramatic picture of every day."[28] In the words of another Christian professor and writer, "The challenge of [Jesus'] unexpected prophecies is to accept the transforming rapture ever and again."[29] Many Roman Catholics and mainline denominationalist Protestants hold this view.

- **Preterist:** Like Futurists and Historicists, and unlike Symbolists, Preterists also believe in the literal fulfillment of New Testament prophecy within historical events. However, they believe that most or all New Testament prophecy was fulfilled in the generation of the early church, at the conquest of Jerusalem and destruction of its Temple in A.D. 70. "Partial" preterists believe that the final judgment and resurrection of the dead are still in the future.[30] "Total" or "full" preterists (sometimes called proponents of a "realized eschatology") believe that *all* prophecy, including the Judgment and Resurrection, occurred at the coming of the Lord in judgment against Jerusalem.[31] Sometimes this view is amended with the idea that the "resurrection" of every believer occurs at the time of that believer's death, with death's concomitant release into an eternal spiritual life. "Thus the fulfillment [of biblical prophecy] was in the future from the point of view of the inspired [biblical authors], but it is in the past from our vantage point in history."[32] So the book of Revelation, for example, was written sometime prior to Jerusalem's fall in A.D. 70, rather than at approximately

---

[28] Taken from F.F. Bruce, "Eschatology." *The Evangelical Dictionary of Theology.* Edited by Walter A. Elwell. Grand Rapids, Michigan: Baker Books, 1984: 364.

[29] Robert Jewett, *Jesus Against the Rapture: Seven Unexpected Prophecies.* Philadelphia: Westminster Press, 1979: 142.

[30] For an example of the "partial" preterist position, see Kenneth Gentry's *Before Jerusalem Fell.* Tyler, Texas: Institute for Christian Economics, 1989.

[31] For an example of the "total" preterist position, see Max King's *The Cross and the Parousia of Christ.* Warren, Ohio: Parkman Road Church of Christ, 1986.

[32] Steve Gregg, *Revelation: Four Views*, 2.

A.D. 95 (the date maintained by most Futurists). Noted Christians who favor this early dating include Adam Clarke, J.B. Lightfoot, Philip Schaff, and J. Stuart Russell ("perhaps the most important scholar of the preterist school"[33]), as well as the majority of Bible scholars in the 1800s. Therefore, when New Testament writers spoke of the "soon" return of Christ, they meant it literally—Jesus actually did return within the lifetime of their readers, if we understand his "coming" as a "coming in judgment" to Jerusalem, a judgment against those rejecting Him and a deliverance of those serving Him.

To repeat my previous self-identification, I myself am a "partial" preterist. I believe that most New Testament prophecy was fulfilled in the first-century church, but I also believe in the future Second Coming of Christ, Resurrection of the Dead, and Final Judgment, as described in the Creeds accepted by the historic Church. Since it would be too much of a sideline issue, I will not in this book present the arguments in favor of accepting the historic Creeds, but will simply take such belief as a given amongst orthodox Christians. From here on through-out this book, whenever I use the term "preterist," I am referring to the position known as "partial" preterist. To repeat, therefore: This type of preterist, the "partial" as opposed to the "full" preterist, believes in the future Second Coming of Christ and the future Resurrection of the Dead as described in the Creeds accepted by the historic Church, thus avoiding the charges of "heresy" leveled by some.[34]

For some readers, this may be the very first time they have become aware of these interpretive options. These readers may feel more comfortable with one or two of these options than with the others. However, before they dismiss as "fanciful" any views contrary to their own, they may consider these words: "[N]one of these schools of interpretation can claim any monopoly on scholarship or faith. Each group numbers many fine scholars and devout Christian believers. . . . It is our duty to do the best we can, to study the various systems and accept the view that seems to us right, but always with a certain amount of reservation and of respect for the opinions of others."[35] This seems not only reasonable, but Christian.

---

[33] R.C. Sproul, *The Last Days According to Jesus*. Grand Rapids, Michigan: Baker Book House, 1998: 24.

[34] The full preterist position has been labeled as a "heresy" by, for example, television ministers Jack Van Impe and Perry Stone. The primary reason for this label will be examined in a later chapter.

[35] Albertus Pieters, *The Lamb, the Woman, and the Dragon*. Grand Rapids, Michigan:

However, if all of this discussion be the case, why even bother to make the choice of one interpretive stance over another? All of them seem to have sincere and knowledgeable Christians espousing them. Why choose the preterist position, for instance, over a position such as the futurist, which may be more familiar? In the next chapter, reasons will be presented for choosing "Prophecy Without Panic," the preterist view of biblical prophecy.

Zondervan, 1937: 42.

4. Why Should We Prefer the Preterist View? A Preview of Later Chapters

"I am Alpha and Omega, the beginning and the ending, says the Lord, which is, and which was, and which is to come, the Almighty."—Revelation 1:8.

"The first to speak always seem right, until another comes forward to question him."—Proverbs 18:17 (author's paraphrase).

About 27% of all the verses in the Bible—slightly over a quarter of the entire book—are made up of prophecy in one form or another. Given this, it seems that the interpretive stance we take does make quite a difference in our understanding of the message of the entire Bible. The various books of the Bible are not comprised of isolated passages or stand-alone "proof texts" for this or that doctrine, even though this is the impression left by the way many sermons are constructed. Rather, the Bible forms a coherent interwoven whole, in which the great tapestry of God's redemptive work is revealed. In other words, this debate over differing prophecy interpretations is not merely an academic exercise, helpful perhaps for some studious types, but having no real effect on the typical lives of typical Christians. To the contrary—one's interpretation of biblical prophecy will color how one reads the Bible's messages on God's relationship to history, on Christ's relationship to humanity, and even on God's plan of salvation itself.

As mentioned in the previous chapter, for some readers this may be the very first time they have become aware of the interpretive options of Futurist, Historicist, Symbolist, and Preterist. These readers may feel more comfortable with one or two of these options than with the others, especially if they have been raised and taught solely from the Futurist viewpoint; as the writer of Proverbs tells us, "The first to speak always seem right, until another comes forward to question him" (Proverbs 18:17). However, if this be the case, why choose one interpretive stance over another? Why choose the preterist position, for instance, over a position such as the futurist, which may be more familiar? If all of these interpretations have good arguments for them, why do I think the preterist position is the best of the four discussed and should be adopted?

Some of the reasons given here will be explained more fully in subsequent chapters. For now, however, a simple listing and brief explanation of several reasons will suffice; this chapter, therefore, might be seen as a "preview" of coming attractions. Why should we adopt the preterist interpretation of biblical prophecy? Here are eight quick reasons:

(1) **Jesus taught the preterist interpretation.** Probably the most famous of Jesus' prophecies is found in the Gospel of Matthew, chapters 23-25, especially Chapter 24. In that extended passage, Jesus refers to the destruction of the Jewish Temple: "See ye not all these things [referring to the Temple]? Verily I say unto you, there shall not be left here one stone upon another, that shall not be thrown down" (24:2). His disciples ask Him, "When shall these things be?" (vs. 3). Jesus begins his answer by telling his followers what to expect in the following years, and then comes to his answer to their question: "Verily I say unto you, This generation shall not pass, till all these things be fulfilled" (vs. 34).

Matthew 24 will be discussed more fully in later chapters; for now, it is enough to point out that, despite all the torturous twists and turns futurists attempt with his straightforward answer, Jesus actually expected the fulfillment of his prophecies within one generation. He is not predicting something that is to happen in the far future, but something that would happen within the generation of those hearing Him. Jesus speaks these words in about A.D. 30, and Jerusalem is conquered and the Temple destroyed by the Roman general Titus in the year A.D. 70—within the generation of those then alive, in other words, just as Jesus predicts. His words are fulfilled when the Temple is destroyed and the system of Temple worship ends. Therefore, Jesus Himself taught the preterist position. If He did not, then He, as the all-powerful and all-knowing Son of God, God in the flesh, God the Second Person of the Trinity—was simply *wrong* in his prophetic message.[36] I will

---

[36] "It is clear from the New Testament that they [the apostles] all expected the Second Coming in their own lifetime. And, worse still, they had a reason, and one which you will find very embarrassing. Their Master had told them so. He shared, and indeed created, their delusion. He said in so many words, 'this generation shall not pass until all these things be done.' And he was wrong. He clearly knew no more about the end of the world than anyone else. It is certainly the most embarrassing verse in the Bible."—C.S. Lewis, "The World's Last Night." From

leave futurists to explain how that might be possible. The preterist position makes no such explanation necessary; Jesus was not mistaken, but perfectly and amazingly accurate in his predictions.[37]

(2) **The preterist interpretation explains many of Jesus' more puzzling statements.** If the preterist interpretation were a scientific theory, we would say it has more "explanatory power" than the other theories; that is, it helps to make sense of many more passages of scripture, especially troubling prophetic passages, than the other interpretations do. Let us remain with the Gospel of Matthew for some examples:

"But when they persecute you in this city, flee ye into another: for verily I say unto you, Ye shall not have gone over the cities of Israel, till the Son of man be come" (10:23). It has been nearly 2,000 years since Jesus spoke these words. Surely by now Christians have been able to share the message of Christ with the cities of Israel, wouldn't you think? However, Jesus was not speaking of some event 2,000 years in his disciples' future; rather, He was speaking of his soon "coming in judgment" against Jerusalem, which occurred within the generation of those hearing Him. He was, therefore, warning his followers that their time of witness to Israel was limited. Note that when this verse is understood in the preterist fashion, the apparent difficulty of it disappears. The same is true of the following passages as well.

"Verily I say unto you, There be some standing here, which shall not taste of death, till they see the Son of man coming in his kingdom" (16:28). This is the final verse of Chapter 16 of Matthew's Gospel; most futurists therefore relate it to the opening

---

The World's Last Night and Other Essays. New York: Harcourt Brace Jovanovich, reprinted 1960: 93-113, p. 98. As much as I admire Lewis and his work, of course I completely disagree with him on this point. In his defense, perhaps he had heard only the futurist interpretation of this passage, in which case his mistake is understandable.

[37] "Was Jesus mistaken? Should we feel uncomfortable because the world is still with us almost two thousand years after he prophesied its frightful end? A closer look at Jesus' words in the context of ancient Judaism reveals a better interpretation. Namely, Jesus was predicting the demise of the Jerusalem Temple—the architectural symbol of the Old Covenant. . . . From this perspective Jesus stands vindicated, since his words did come to pass within the lifetime of his contemporaries."—Scott Hahn and Curtis Mitch, "End of the World?" *The Ignatius Catholic Study Bible*, 2nd edition. Revised Standard Version. San Francisco: Ignatius Press, 2010: 50.

episode of Chapter 17, which occurs about a week later. Jesus takes Peter, James, and John up a mountainside and is transfigured before them (the "Mount of Transfiguration" passage). Moses and Elijah then appear with the glorified Christ and speak with Him regarding his coming death. Since Moses and Elijah, representing the Law and the Prophets of the Old Testament, appear with Jesus in glory, many futurists think of this as the fulfillment of Jesus' prophecy a week earlier of his "coming in his kingdom."

However, we should note what the prophecy actually says: that there were "some" standing with Jesus "who would not taste of death" until "they see the Son of man coming in his kingdom." Was Jesus speaking to a group of extremely old or sick people who were all close to death—so close that they might not even live over the following week? If He was referring only to Peter, James, and John, were they all quite close to death as well? The obvious answer is no, because He was not prophesying regarding an event (the Transfiguration) which happened only a week later. Jesus was predicting an event which was to occur about forty years later, in A.D. 70, the conquest of Jerusalem by the Romans. When this is understood, the rest of the verse is understood as well. Over the next forty years, some of those hearing Christ *would* die, but some would still remain to see the prophesied "coming" occur, when Jesus came as Judge of the nation that had rejected Him.[38] The same is true of the next passage, which takes place during Jesus' mock trial before his death:

"And the high priest arose, and said unto him, Answerest thou nothing? What is it which these witness against thee? But Jesus held his peace. And the high priest answered and said unto him, I adjure thee by the living God, that thou tell us whether thou be the Christ, the Son of God. Jesus saith

---

[38] On this verse, an extremely puzzling comment has been made by futurist author Ron Rhodes, in his book *Five-Minute Apologetics for Today* (Eugene, Oregon: Harvest House, 2010). He writes of this verse, "Jesus had in mind His transfiguration—a preview of the glory of the kingdom—which happened one week later (Matthew 17:1-13). Supporting this view is the fact that some of the disciples standing there were no longer alive by AD 70" (p. 322). But isn't this exactly what Jesus predicted, that some of those hearing Him would be alive and some dead? In what way does this validate the futurist position? Does not the comment rather support the preterist view of a fulfillment a few decades into the future, when some of Jesus' followers would already be dead, not the futurist view of a fulfillment a week later?

unto him, Thou hast said: nevertheless I say unto you, Hereafter shall ye see the Son of man sitting on the right hand of power, and coming in the clouds of heaven" (26:62-64). Again, Jesus' reply to the direct question is best understood given the preterist interpretation of it, since He says to some of those listening that they themselves would see the Son "coming in the clouds of heaven." Old Testament prophets used the phrase "coming in the clouds" as a picture of the Lord's coming in judgment, not as a gracious coming in mercy, and Jesus' hearers would have understood the phrase in that way. Essentially Jesus is repeating what He had already said earlier: that some of those listening to Him would still be alive to see the coming judgment of Jerusalem.

Many other scriptural passages could be adduced to support this particular point, that the preterist position better explains many puzzling New Testament sayings. However, perhaps these three are enough for the point to be made. What other reasons are there to adopt the preterist view?

(3) **The preterist interpretation answers the question, "What did the earliest Christians think of biblical prophecy?"** Often in the New Testament, comments are made and commands given which make much more sense given the preterist interpretation of Jesus' prophecies, prophecies the early Christians would have known well. For example, in his First Epistle to the Corinthians, Paul the Apostle gives extended advice regarding the advisability of marriage and concludes: "I say therefore to the unmarried and widows, It is good for them if they abide even as I [that is, unmarried]" (7:8). After some discussion of those who are already married, Paul refers to "the present distress": "I suppose therefore that this is good for the present distress, I say, that it is good for a man so to be. Art thou bound to a wife? Seek not to be loosed. Art thou loosed from a wife? Seek not a wife. [If some do marry] such shall have trouble in the flesh: but I spare you. But this I say, brethren, the time is short. . . . for the fashion of this world is passing away" (26-31) Paul definitely is not writing against marriage as such; he simply is pointing out that given the distressing circumstances of the Roman occupation, and given the shortness of time before the world known by the early Christians would be "passing away," it would be better to remain unmarried. Many potential anxieties and troublesome circumstances could thus be

31

avoided entirely by unmarried Christians, not preoccupied with the welfare of a spouse, when the coming of Christ in judgment against their known world occurred. Note that Paul's teaching on marriage is not the point at issue here; rather, the point is his understanding of the "distress" coming soon upon the world the early Christians knew.

Another example comes from Eusebius Pamphilus, the author of the earliest known full-length Christian history outside of the Bible itself (his "Ecclesiastical History," finished around the year 326). Eusebius describes how the Emperor Vespasian, who "had become illustrious in the campaign against the Jews" as a general in the Jewish/Roman War, returns to Rome and "commits the care of the war against the Jews into the hands of his son Titus." After depicting the horrors of the famine in Jerusalem following from the Roman siege of the city in A.D. 70, Eusebius adds, "To these accounts it may be proper to add the sure prediction of our Savior, in which He foretold these very events." He then quotes from Jesus' prophecies of Matthew 24 and summarizes as follows: "All this occurred in this manner, in the second year of the reign of Vespasian, according to the predictions of our Lord and Savior Jesus Christ, who by his divine power foresaw all these things as if already present at the time, who wept and mourned indeed at the prospect, as the holy evangelists show in their writings [the Gospels]. . . . On comparing the declarations of our Savior with the other parts of the historian's work, where he describes the whole war, how can one fail to acknowledge and wonder at the truly divine and extraordinary foreknowledge and prediction of our Savior?"[39] Indeed, Jesus' predictions do cause us to acknowledge and wonder at his amazingly accurate words—but only when they are interpreted from the preterist point of view, as referring to the judgment and conquest of Jerusalem. This interpretation of biblical prophecy is not subject to the wild, feverish speculations and fantasies of end-times enthusiasts; it is subject rather to *what actually happened* in history, as is detailed by Eusebius, Josephus, and other historians.

Thus the preterist interpretation of prophecy gives us a greater continuity with the early Church, a greater sense of an unbroken,

---

[39] Eusebius Pamphilus, *Ecclesiastical History*. Grand Rapids, Michigan: Baker Book House, reprinted 1993. Book III, Chapters 5-7: 85-93.

continuous heritage and living past. The Book of Revelation describes Jesus as He "who is, who was, and who is to come" (1:8). When we examine how the earliest Christians interpreted his prophecies, we not only see Him as the one who "is to come," but as the one who "was" a marvelous and true Prophet and who "is" the Judge of all nations.

(4) **The preterist interpretation fits better with Old Testament prophecy, as entire themes of Scripture begin to open up to us**. Recently a fellow Christian said to me, "Context, context! All you want to talk about is context. To me, what is important in the Bible is the spiritual meaning I get out of different verses. Isn't that important, too?" To this I replied, "Yes, certainly the spiritual meaning you receive individually is important to your spiritual growth and your relationship with God. But I would feel much better about the 'spiritualized' interpretations of biblical passages if the people offering them also seem to understand the passages' plain and straightforward meaning as well."

Along this line, a curious phenomenon seems to take place in many Christians' lives: They know the Bible very well; they can quote it and answer many questions about various verses and passages. They can even relate it to their personal lives and the struggles, sorrows, joys, and triumphs they undergo. However, they are somehow biblically illiterate when it comes to *overall themes*. For example, they find it difficult to answer questions such as "To whom was this book written? What were they facing? What was the historical context? What did it mean to the original hearers or readers?" Probably many Christians find this difficult because these questions are rarely addressed from the pulpits of their churches. Most preaching is more "topical" than exegetical.

However, biblical messages such as those found in the prophecies of the Old Testament suddenly open up and make much more sense when we take into account their historical context. For example, Isaiah writes to the northern kingdom of Israel and warns them (in my paraphrase): "You have rejected God, and He is bringing judgment upon you in the form of the Assyrians; they will overcome you. However, the Assyrians will not conquer the southern kingdom of Judah; in fact, Assyria will be judged and conquered itself by the Babylonians. But do not rejoice too much, Judeans of the south; you also have rejected God, and the same civilization that conquers the Assyrians will be the one to conquer you." The extended passages in Isaiah which could otherwise be confusing or distracting clear up remarkably when this overall theme of the book is kept in mind. Furthermore, the prophet Jeremiah then steps up, over a century later, and tells the southern kingdom: "Surrender now, so that you might live; the conquerors of which Isaiah prophesied (the Babylonians) God is now going to use to conquer you. You will go into captivity for a long time in Babylon—such a long time you can build houses, plant trees, have children—but you will eventually return to this place, your homeland." Ezekiel and Daniel then write of this "Babylonian Captivity"; in fact, Daniel lives long enough to also write of the Medo-Persian takeover of the Babylonians. Daniel surviving his ordeal in the lions' den, and the three Jewish friends surviving their ordeal in the fiery furnace, are pictures of the Jewish people surviving their ordeal in the "lions' den" of the Babylonian Captivity.

We see a pattern or motif emerging here: First, Israel rejects God and God's Law; secondly, God then uses a powerful Gentile force to bring judgment upon Israel; finally, Israel is not abandoned by God, but is preserved through persecution and captivity. The other prophetic books of the Old Testament similarly make much more sense as this repeated pattern or motif becomes apparent.

The preterist interpretation of New Testament prophecy also fits in well with this overarching narrative of persecution and preservation found in the Old Testament. In the New Testament, Israel as a whole rejects God once more in the sense of rejecting God in the flesh, the Son of God, the Messiah. Next, the Lord Christ Himself, as King and Judge, uses a powerful Gentile force (the Romans) to bring judgment upon Israel and specifically upon Jerusalem. However, this does not mean the Jewish people are abandoned; to the contrary, they are preserved even into the present day.

We can see that entire themes of the prophetic scriptures become strikingly clear as we approach the Bible in this way. Further, the New and Old Testaments can be seen as a linked and congruent set of stories both of God's judgment and of his salvation.

(5) **The writer of the Book of Revelation agrees with the preterist interpretation.** The Apostle John in the Book of Revelation is so repetitive on one certain point, it seems incredible that we glide over it so easily in our reading. The point is simply this: He clearly

predicts Jesus' return in the very near future to his first-century readers, not a return to come centuries later. In the opening verse of Revelation, he writes that his prophecies "must shortly come to pass" (1:1). He writes that "the time is at hand" (1:3). Jesus Himself says, "Behold, I come quickly" (3:11; 22:7, 12) and "Surely I come quickly" (22:20). Some futurists interpret these passages as meaning that Jesus is coming "in a quick manner" or "swiftly" when He finally does come, which seems entirely to negate the sense of urgency implied. At any rate, such an interpretation cannot account for the time being "at hand" (Greek *eggus* or *eng-goos*), which means *near, soon, at the door.*

If John were warning believers of Jesus' soon return in judgment, this would entail that the Book of Revelation was written sometime just prior to the conquest of Jerusalem and destruction of the Temple, a timing which is disputed by many biblical scholars.[40] Fortunately, John himself does not leave us in doubt on the matter: In Revelation itself, he writes of a horrible beast with seven heads before immediately telling us that the seven heads are "seven mountains" and "seven kings." The city on seven mountains is Rome itself; of the seven kings John writes, "Five are fallen, and one is, and the other is not yet come; and when he cometh, he must continue a short space" (17:10). The five leaders of Rome who "are fallen" are Julius Caesar, Augustus Caesar, Tiberius Caesar, Caligula Caesar, and Claudius Caesar, all of whom had already died much previously. The seventh king who rules only "a short space" is Galba Caesar, who only rules about seven months. The sixth ruler in between—the one of whom John says "one is" (in other words, is alive while John is writing)—is Nero Caesar, who dies in A.D. 68. Therefore, if Nero is still alive while John is writing the Book of Revelation, then John's prophecies of the soon coming of Jesus are written just before the cataclysmic events of A.D. 70. This, of course, fits perfectly with the preterist interpretation of these events.

(6) **The preterist interpretation spares Christians the embarrassment, especially in today's instant-media atmosphere, of our continuously mistaken predictions regarding the Lord's Coming.** This is probably the weakest of all of these arguments,

---

[40] For a good discussion of this point, see Kenneth Gentry's *Before Jerusalem Fell* (1989).

but many Christians might feel it emotionally as the strongest. It is certainly the case that many, many Christians have brought much discredit and disrepute upon the Church as a whole by their continual acceptance of Rapture predictions, their continual back-pedaling attempts at explanation when it doesn't happen, and their continual acceptance of the next Rapture predictions (often by the very same ministers!) that come down the road. We must seek never to discredit the Body of Christ and the Lord's work by our reckless and undisciplined speculations.[41]

(7) **The futurist position does not seem to allow us to appreciate the very language of biblical prophecy, while the preterist position actually requires us to do so.** Biblical prophets, especially those working in the "apocalyptic" tradition (from the Greek *apocalupsis*, "revelation"), often speak and write in meta-phoric language that is so striking it is even bizarre and nightmarish. For example, the prophets often write of stars falling from the heavens, disturbances in the sun and moon, the Lord coming in the clouds, and so on. However, futurists usually take this language as intended literally, and so they examine heavenly portents such as comets, solar and lunar eclipses, "blood moons," and so on. They then point out that these atmospheric events have not yet occurred in the literal sense, and so the preterist interpretation of much prophecy as already fulfilled must be mistaken. Preterists, on the other hand, think that when under-stood biblically, these events *have* already occurred. When we read these words as the authors intended them, we are better able to see what they actually signify. The subject of the Lord coming in the clouds will be covered in a later chapter; for now, let us consider the language of heavenly disturbances.

The disturbances of the sun, moon, and stars are common images found in the prophets. "In the prophetic language, great commotions upon earth are often represented under the notion of commotions and changes in the heavens"[42]:

---

[41] There are many instances of this debunking and mocking on the part of non-Christians taking place in today's media. For one example, see Matthew J. Sharps, Schuyler W. Liao, and Megan R. Herrera, "Remembrance of Apocalypse Past: The Psychology of True Believers When Nothing Happens." *Skeptical Inquirer* 38.6 (Nov./Dec. 2014): 54-58. The illustration accompanying this article shows a person holding a sign reading "The End Is Near (Next Time)." It is easy to become upset and irritated at this skepticism; however, by now don't these skeptics have a point?

- The fall of Babylon is represented by the stars and constellations of heaven withdrawing their light, and the sun and moon being darkened (Isaiah 13:9-10).
- The destruction of Egypt is represented by the heaven being covered, the sun enveloped with a cloud, and the moon withholding her light (Ezekiel 32:7-8).
- The coming of the Assyrians into Israel is represented by the sun going down at noon and darkness on a clear day (Amos 8:9).
- The persecution of the Jews by Antiochus Epiphanes is represented by casting down some of the host of heaven and the stars to the ground (Daniel 8:10).
- The very destruction of Jerusalem is represented by the prophet Joel (Joel 2:30-31) by showing wonders in heaven and in earth—darkening the sun, and turning the moon into blood.

"This general mode of describing these judgments leaves no room to doubt the propriety of its application in the present case [i.e., in Matthew 24]."[43] The Lord coming in the clouds, the sun, moon, and stars being darkened, the powers of the heavens being shaken—all this took place at the Lord's coming in judgment upon Jerusalem, in A.D. 70. These prophecies are not a sort of literal weather report; they are a warning of judgment. Preterists, given their understanding of biblical prophecy, are able to understand this apocalyptic language for what it actually signifies, while the futurist position is forced to misrepresent this language.

All of the futurists I know personally are good, honorable, devout, and intelligent Christians, and of course they are not *trying* to misrepresent Jesus' words. However, it is required by their interpretive position to see these events as still in the future, and thus to see them literally. It is really far past time that we stop thinking of these prophecies as an account of highly unusual weather conditions which have not yet occurred, and start reading them in light of the entire biblical prophetic tradition.

---

[42] This quotation and the following biblical examples are taken from Adam Clarke, *Commentary on Matthew*. In *Parallel Classic Commentary on the New Testament*. Edited by Mark Water. Chattanooga, Tennessee: AMG Publishers, 2004: 343.

[43] Ibid., p. 343.

(8) **The preterist interpretation helps make us aware of what the Church is supposed to be doing right now.** At a time somewhat late in his ministry, Jesus utters an entire series of parables with roughly the same point. One brief example will serve to illustrate:

> Another parable spake he unto them; The kingdom of heaven is like unto leaven, which a woman took, and hid in three measures of meal, till the whole was leavened. (Matthew 13:33)

The "kingdom of heaven" in Matthew's Gospel is spoken of as the "kingdom of God" in the others; there is really no difference between the two phrases except that Matthew uses the one to avoid offending his Jewish readers by the constant use of the name of God. Therefore, if we substitute the phrase "Kingdom of God" for the other, Jesus says here that the Kingdom of God, which is "among us," is like leaven transforming everything around it until all its surroundings are touched by its expansive influence and changed for the better. For those committed to the futurist position, this parable and the others like it in Matthew 13 can make very little sense. Because these parables show the picture of God's kingdom as it spreads out and infiltrates its surroundings until the surroundings are transformed by its power, they do not fit in well with the picture of a Church being lifted out by the Rapture from the midst of a world sold out and given over to evil and error. In fact, we simply cannot "lift out" leaven from the dough into which it has been mixed. Many futurists therefore interpret this verse as showing the action of *evil* within the Church itself, leading to a more and more corrupt and ineffective Church, until the Kingdom of God (in the form of the Rapture) finally arrives and straightens everything up.[44]

But the leaven does not represent evil here; it represents *teaching*, the presentation of the Word of God to the surrounding world. As Jesus tells his disciples at another time, "leaven" represents "doctrine" (Matthew 16:6-12). In that specific case, the leaven is the corrupt doctrine of the Pharisees; in this case under discussion, the leaven is the doctrine of the Kingdom of God; but the important point is that in both cases the use of the word "leaven"

---

[44] For example, see Scofield's footnote to this verse, in which he says: "Leaven is the principle of corruption working subtly; is invariably used in a bad sense." To this one can only respond that leaven is sometimes used in a bad sense *except* when (as here) it is not.

shows the influence of *teaching*, not of *evil*. Teaching can be evil, but teaching can also be helpful, positive, and life-transforming; as Jesus says, "The kingdom of heaven is like unto leaven." How futurists can go from this statement to saying that the leaven represents evil and contamination is beyond me. The kingdom of heaven is like unto evil and contamination? How does that make sense? [45]

In fact, there are two main differences here between the futurist view and the preterist view of these parables: (1) Futurists are *waiting* to be snatched out by God *from* the world (by the Rapture), while preterists are *working* with God *to change* the world (by the Gospel), since preterists are not bunkered down hoping for rescue. In the futurist view, no matter how evil and error-filled the world becomes, that is just fine; after the Rapture, the world will get everything it deserves in God's fiery judgment. In the preterist view, no matter how evil and error-filled the world becomes, there is still hope; once the Church actually accepts its mission of being the leaven mixed by God into the loaf, actively out to transform the world around us by the message of God's saving Word, we can help to change the evil and error in the world through the power of Christ. (2) The second difference is tied to the first: The futurist looks forward to a sweeping and dramatic and sudden instantiation of the Kingdom of God, while the preterist takes these parabolic pictures as Jesus presented them: as leaven, for example, patiently and quietly and confidently working underground, behind the scenes, hidden in the loaf, until the whole is changed by the power of the Gospel. "First the blade, then the ear, then the full corn in the ear" is how the Kingdom arrives, steadily and gradually, according to Jesus (Mark 4:26-28). He does not say the Kingdom arrives like the 82nd Airborne, bursting on the scene to lift the beaten-down elect out of all their problems.

Many other reasons besides these eight could be listed for accepting the preterist interpretation, but these will do for now. (One would think that the first reason by itself should be enough for a Christian.) Some of these given here, as well as others, will be explored more thoroughly in the pages to come, but for now, here is a quick recapitulation. We should accept the preterist interpretation of biblical prophecy for these reasons:

---

[45] Perhaps this would be a good place to mention that I am grateful that the actual Christian *lives* of the futurists I know are much, much better than their end-times doctrine.

(1) Jesus taught the preterist interpretation.

(2) Further, the preterist interpretation explains many of Jesus' more puzzling statements.

(3) To carry on the central theme of "Prophecy Without Panic," the preterist interpretation answers the question, "What did the earliest Christians think of biblical prophecy?"

(4) The preterist interpretation also fits better with Old Testament prophecy, as entire themes of Scripture begin to open up to us.

(5) Even the writer of the Book of Revelation agrees with the preterist interpretation.

(6) On a more personal note, the preterist interpretation spares Christians the embarrassment, especially in today's instant-media atmosphere, of our continuously mistaken predictions regarding the Lord's Coming.

(7) Interestingly, and helpfully for our reading of the Bible, the futurist position does not seem to allow us to appreciate the very language of biblical prophecy, while the preterist position actually requires us to do so.

(8) And finally, the preterist interpretation helps make us aware of what the Church is supposed to be doing right now, as will be explained more fully in this book's very last chapter.

5. What Are the "End Times"?

Are We Living in the End Times?—contemporary book title.
Are We Living in the Time of the End?—contemporary book title.
Are We Living in the Last Days?—contemporary book title.

When one seeks to understand the biblical answer to the question, "What are the 'end times'?" corollary questions also pop up. These questions include, "Are we living in the end times now?" and "What will the end times be like?" As a teacher of a course on the Bible in a secular state college, I hear these questions often, even from students who are not openly professing Christians. These students are familiar with the term "end times" even if they know nothing else about the Bible, for they have picked it up from numerous horror films with "end of days" or apocalyptic themes, from discussions they have heard or overheard between Christians, and even from many currently popular television shows, such as *Supernatural* and *The Living Dead*. These students often ask me personally, "Do you think we are living in the end times now?" My response, which usually opens up some lively and profitable class discussion, is always the same; I always say, "If I tell you, you won't understand what I'm saying." When the students pressure me, I repeat, "Well, all right, I'll tell you; however, I am warning you in advance that you will not understand the answer." After a dramatic pause, I tell them: "The answer is *yes*."

The reason these non-professing students do not understand that positive answer to the question is the same reason many openly Bible-believing Christians also would not understand it: They have asked the question with certain preconceptions in mind. Primarily, they think they already understand what the phrase "end times" actually means. Due to these preconceptions, often my students are startled as we go through the New Testament itself and read all the numerous passages that refer to the subject and which help explain how we are to understand "the end times." Here, for example, the writer of the Book of Hebrews explains:

God, who at sundry times and in diverse manners spake in time past unto the fathers by the prophets, hath *in these last days* spoken

unto us by his Son, whom he hath appointed heir of all things, by
whom also he made the worlds. (Hebrews 1:1-2, emphasis added)

So when did the last days actually begin? God has spoken through many
people and in many ways in the past, the author of Hebrews writes. He has
dealt with the peoples and nations of the world at many times, as well as
with individuals; he "did not leave Himself without witness" (Acts 14:17),
even in pre-Christian times, and even in the epochs before any of the Bible
was written down. However, in this passage from Hebrews, it seems clear
that God has now *with finality* spoken by revealing Himself in human form.
In other words, the Incarnate Son of God, Jesus, the One who was to
come, is God's final Word on the subject of salvation and humanity's final
end.

We should therefore see that *the end times began when Jesus arrived*—and we
have been living in the end times ever since. The Christian Church is God's
objective witness in the world to his end-time dealings with humanity. To
quote again from Hebrews, "Now once *in the end of the world* hath he [Jesus]
appeared to put away sin by the sacrifice of himself" (9:26, emphasis
added). We have been in the time of "the end of the world" for 2,000 years
now. God can do no more for us than to offer Himself—which He has
already done.

"But that's not what I mean," someone might object. "When I refer to
the end times, I am speaking of the end of the world and the cataclysmic
end of our age. That's what 'end times' means to me, not merely the time of
Jesus' arrival here on earth." However, we should not be asking ourselves
what the term "end times" means to us, but rather what it meant to the
writers of the New Testament. To them, the arrival of the Son of God was
not a "mere" event, but rather a cataclysm that split human history, the
eruption of God into his creation. Paradoxically, this "cataclysm," this
"eruption," took place in the form of a powerless baby born into a
nondescript locale.

Given this truth, in the biblical writings, the many references to "the
end" generally do not mean the end of the world, but rather the end of a
civilization, a nation, a time period, or even a city; "the end" usually refers
to a way of doing things that is coming to a close. It refers to events "that
may be closer to the writer's time than to the end of human history."[46] In
the New Testament, it refers to the time that God begins to deal with the

---

46 "End Times." *Dictionary of Biblical Imagery.* Edited by L. Ryken, J.C. Wilhoit, and
T. Longman III. Downers Grove, Illinois: IVP Press, 1998: 231.

human race through Jesus, not through the Temple sacrifices or any other such system.

When understood in that light, other examples abound throughout the Scriptures. "The time is at hand," writes John in Revelation (1:3). In one of his other writings, John asserts that Christians are already living "in the last time": "Little children, it is the last time: and as ye have heard that antichrist shall come, even now are there many antichrists; whereby we know that it is the last time" (1 John 2:18). Jesus teaches his followers, "The hour is coming, *and now is*, when the dead shall hear the voice of the Son of God: and they that hear shall live" (John 5:25, emphasis added). Paul the Apostle writes to his spiritual son, Timothy, and tells him, "This know also, that in the last days perilous times shall come." He then goes on to describe the type of persons existing "in the last days" and finishes by telling Timothy, "From such turn away" (2 Timothy 3:1-5); in other words, these sorts of "last-days" persons were in existence during the lives of Paul and Timothy themselves. Paul is confident, however: "But they shall proceed no further" (vs. 9). In his First Epistle to the Corinthians, Paul further writes that certain events in Jewish history "happened unto them for examples: and they are written for our admonition, *upon whom the ends of the world are come*" (10:11, emphasis added).

Other New Testament writers express similar ideas. The Apostle Peter declares that we are "redeemed . . . with the precious blood of Christ, as of a lamb without blemish and without spot: who verily was foreordained before the foundation of the world, but was manifest *in these last times* for you" (1 Peter 1:18-20, emphasis added). Later in the same epistle Peter writes, "But the end of all things is at hand: be ye therefore sober, and watch unto prayer" (4:7). Likewise, the elder James sternly warns those among the rich who are living unjustly, "Go to now, ye rich men, weep and howl for your miseries that shall come upon you. . . . Ye have heaped treasure together for the last days" (James 5:1-3). Even in the brief Epistle of Jude, the author mentions the prophetic timeframe: "Remember the words [of the apostles], that they told you there should be mockers in the last time" (vss. 17-18). Lest the readers think of this as purely a future occurrence, Jude then immediately says, "These be they who separate themselves, sensual, having not the Spirit" (vs. 19). We see, then, that according to Jude the "mockers in the last time" were already among the Church in the first century; therefore, the first-century Church was already "in the last time."

When did the end times or last days begin? As we have seen, according to the writings of John, Paul, Peter, James, Jude, the author of Hebrews, and in the words of Jesus Himself, the end times or last days began with the advent of Jesus Christ. And, since God has not changed his method of dealing with humanity since that time, we are still in the end times today.

Occasionally one hears the rebuttal, "Perhaps the early Christians did consider the 'last days' and 'end times' to have begun with the life of Jesus. However, all that means is that we are now living in 'the last of the last days,' the 'end of the end times.'" The problem with this frequently-heard declaration is simply that those phrases are found nowhere in the Bible. Nor are they supported with any biblical evidence. They are simply asserted in the attempt to help maintain the futurist position by pushing "the last days" off into our future.

So what are the end times? Are we living in the end times now? When considered from the biblical point of view, we can now understand the answer; the answer is simply *yes*. However, this answer has nothing to do with prophecies of gloom and doom. God has now spoken with finality by revealing Himself in human form, by taking on our human flesh and condition. The Son of God, Jesus Christ, is God's final Word on the subject of salvation and humanity's final end. We should therefore see that *the end times began when Jesus arrived*—and we have been living in the end times ever since. The Christian Church is God's objective witness in the world to his end-time dealings with humanity, right now and for the past two millennia. From this perspective of God's salvation history, the idea of "the end times" is not a cause for apprehension or panic, but rather a cause for deep rejoicing and thanksgiving for the salvation of the world.

6. Matthew 24 (Part 1): When Did the Whole World Hear the Gospel?

"According to the modern consensus, Jesus thought the eschatological judgment to be near. Recent attempts to deny this do not persuade."[47]

I would like to present the following three chapters a bit differently. I am reasonably confident that most of the readers of this book are more aware of the futurist dispensationalist position than of any other; not only is it the best known in America, but it is also the most "noticeable." It is a teaching that gets headlines: "Christians Say Rapture Will Occur This September" grabs the attention much more readily than "Christians Say All History Is Part of God's Plan" or "Christians Say Prophecies Fulfilled in A.D. 70: Massive Amounts of Detailed, Small-Print Argument to Follow." Even non-Christians would think the second headline to be rather banal, while the third would cause immediate glazing-over of the eyes. So, since the futurist position is already fairly well known, in this chapter and the two following I want to allow the preterist position to speak for itself. Let's imagine a conversation between a futurist and a preterist. As the preterist position will require more background explanation, I will let the preterist do most of the talking, with the futurist making comments and offering criticisms.

A focal point of interpretive dispute among biblical prophecy experts is the Olivet Discourse, Jesus' words as recorded in Matthew 24 and its parallel passages, Mark 13 and Luke 17 and 21. An analysis of this one prophecy might be enough to get a taste of the differences in the two interpretive stances. Therefore, this imagined conversation will revolve around the single chapter of Matthew 24, the verses of which I will interpolate as needed. Also, since a few different questions arise in this discussion,

---

[47] D.C. Allison, Jr. "Eschatology." *Dictionary of Jesus and the Gospels*. Edited by J.B. Green, S. McKnight, and I.H. Marshall. Downers Grove, Illinois: InterVarsity Press, 1992: 207.

questions which deserve separate attention, this conversation is going to take place over three consecutive chapters focusing on different topics. Here begins Part 1:

[1] And Jesus went out, and departed from the temple: and his disciples came to him to show him the buildings of the temple.

[2] And Jesus said unto them, See ye not all these things? Verily I say unto you, There shall not be left here one stone upon another, that shall not be thrown down.

[3] And as he sat upon the mount of Olives, the disciples came unto him privately, saying, Tell us, when shall these things be? And what shall be the sign of thy coming, and of the end of the world?

Preterist: It seems like a simple enough question.

Futurist: But it is not. If you'll notice, there are actually two questions. "The order is as follows: 'When shall these things be?'—i.e., destruction of the Temple and city. . . . The remainder of Matthew 24:3 really constitutes a single question: 'And what shall be the sign of thy coming, and of the end of the age [*aion*, translated as "world" in the King James Version]?' The answer [to this second question] is in verses 4-33."[48] So Jesus' followers are asking Him to explain first of all what He meant by saying the Temple would be destroyed; secondly, they are asking Jesus to reveal the signs of his future coming. Matthew 24 answers two separate questions, in other words. One question's answer (the destruction of the Temple) has already occurred in history, while the other's (the coming of Jesus) is yet to come.

Preterist: There are at least a couple of reasons I would not accept your argument. First, the disciples do not seem to be concerned with a coming of Christ in the far future—this is really one question, not two. When Jesus tells them the Temple will be destroyed, they respond rather naturally by assuming the destruction of the Temple is an act of judgment by the coming Messiah, Who is standing in front of them. The "end of the age" is not the end of all history, but the end of the Jewish system of Temple worship and sacrifice. Worship is from henceforth to center around the new Temple, Jesus' body, broken and raised up in three days (John 2:18-21). The Temple's destruction, the Messiah's coming in judgment on Jerusalem, and the end of the Temple age—all of these events are wrapped up in one question with one answer: "When shall these things be?"

Secondly, I wouldn't accept your argument because Jesus gives the disciples a very straightforward, literal answer to their single question. They

---

[48] C.I. Scofield. Footnote to Matthew 24:3, *New Scofield Reference Bible*. New York: Oxford University Press, 1967.

ask when these things will happen. He begins answering them by telling them what to expect, and then summarizes in verse 34: "Verily I say unto you, This generation shall not pass, till all these things be fulfilled." He tells them that all the prophecies of Matthew 24, at least up to verse 34, will be fulfilled in their generation.

Futurist: No, the "generation" Jesus is talking about in verse 34 is not the generation of people then living. It is either (1) the generation of people seeing the Rapture, or more likely (2) the "race" of Jews (from the Greek *genea*). He is simply saying that the Jews *as a people* would not pass away until all these prophecies were fulfilled, despite all the intense persecutions of the Jewish *genea*. "The record of history validates our Lord's words. For the Jews have survived despite the Torquemadas, the Hitlers, the Stalins, and the Eichmanns."[49] The Jewish people will still be around to see the fulfillment of Jesus' words; that is what He is saying to them.

Preterist: That seems a very strained and unnatural reading of that verse. If Jesus were referring to the Jews as a people, He would have used the Greek word *genos*, not *genea*. Everywhere else in Matthew's Gospel, *genea* is used for the generation then alive. For example, from the previous chapter:

> Verily I say unto you, all these things shall come upon *this generation*. O Jerusalem, Jerusalem, thou that killest the prophets and stonest them that are sent unto thee, how often would I have gathered thy children together . . . and ye would not! Behold, your house is left unto you desolate. (Matthew 23:36-38, emphasis added)

" 'This generation' is a recurring phrase in the Bible, and each time it is used it bears the ordinary sense of the people belonging to one fairly comprehensive age group. . . . Jesus' hearers could have understood Him to mean only that 'all these things' would take place within *their* generation. Not only does 'generation' in the phrase 'this generation' always mean the people alive at one particular time; the phrase itself always means 'the generation now living.'"[50]

If we understand the "coming" of the Lord as a coming in judgment to those who rejected Him, then verse 34 carries a literal meaning. Jesus spoke these words in about A.D. 30, and Jerusalem and the Temple are destroyed by the Roman general Titus beginning with the extensive siege of A.D. 70—within the generation of those then alive, in other words, just as Jesus

---

[49] Dr. Walter Martin, *Essential Christianity: A Handbook of Basic Christian Doctrines.* Revised edition. Ventura, California: Regal Books, 1980: 97.

[50] F.F. Bruce, *The Hard Sayings of Jesus.* From *Hard Sayings of the Bible.* W.C. Kaiser, Jr.; P.H. Davids; F.F. Bruce; and M.T. Brauch. Downers Grove, Illinois: Inter-Varsity Press, 1996: 446.

predicted. "Forty years is not too long a period to be called a generation; in fact, forty years is the conventional length of a generation in the biblical vocabulary."[51] This also explains a later incident: "As Jesus bears his cross to Calvary He exhorts the 'daughters of Jerusalem' to weep for themselves because of the coming judgment."[52] He has already predicted what is going to happen *to them*, not to a generation in the distant future.

In fact, He has already told his followers the exact same thing previously, that the generation hearing Him would be the generation seeing his coming: "But when they persecute you in this city, flee ye into another: for verily I say unto you, Ye shall not have gone over the cities of Israel, till the Son of man be come" (Matthew 10:23). Doesn't that sound like a literal prediction of a first-century return of Christ?

Futurist: There are several problems with your literal reading of verse 34 and "this generation." However, in order to highlight these problems, we'll have to look at some more selections from Matthew 24 itself.

Preterist: All right.

[4] And Jesus answered and said unto them, Take heed that no man deceive you.

[5] For many shall come in my name, saying, I am Christ; and shall deceive many.

[6] And ye shall hear of wars and rumors of wars: see that ye be not troubled: for all these things must come to pass, but the end is not yet.

[7] For nation shall rise against nation, and kingdom against kingdom: and there shall be famines, and pestilences, and earthquakes, in diverse places.

[8] All these are the beginning of sorrows.

[9] Then shall they deliver you up to be afflicted, and shall kill you: and ye shall be hated of all nations for my name's sake.

[10] And then shall many be offended, and shall betray one another, and shall hate one another.

[11] And many false prophets shall rise, and shall deceive many.

[12] And because iniquity shall abound, the love of many shall wax cold.

[13] But he that shall endure unto the end, the same shall be saved.

[14] And this gospel of the kingdom shall be preached in all the world for a witness unto all nations; and then shall the end come.

---

[51] Ibid., p. 447.
[52] Kenneth Gentry, *Before Jerusalem Fell*, p. 130.

Futurist: Here's the first problem with your view that Matthew 24 is for the most part fulfilled in the first century church: Look at verse 14. Has "all the world" heard the gospel preached? Even today, we wouldn't say the entire world has heard the gospel as a witness, and it certainly could not have been true in the first century. What about the peoples of Africa, China, Southeast Asia, and the Americas, just to name a few? When did the first-century apostles preach the gospel to them? So we see that the promise "and then shall the end come" is still to be fulfilled in the future.

Preterist: No, the "end" of which Jesus speaks is still the end of Temple worship at the destruction of Jerusalem under Titus.

Futurist: Your interpretation *cannot* be correct, as I've already pointed out, because the whole world could not have heard the gospel in the first century of the church.

Preterist: Yes, it did.

Futurist: Okay, now you're joking, right?

Preterist: Not at all. First, the word for "world" that Jesus uses is not the more typical Greek *kosmos* (the ordered creation) or *aion* (age, eon). Rather, He uses *oikoumene*, which means "land" or "the inhabited terrene world." To be even more precise, *oikoumene* means "specifically the Roman Empire," according to Strong's *Concordance*.[53] The same word is used in Luke 2:1, "And it came to pass in those days, that there went out a decree from Caesar Augustus, that *all the world* should be taxed." This certainly does not refer to all the "earth" (South America, Australia, Africa, etc.), but all lands within the purview of the Roman Empire.[54]

In his translation of the New Testament, Kenneth Wuest even renders Matthew 24:14 as "And there shall be proclaimed this good news of the kingdom in the whole Roman Empire." Of course, since Wuest is a futurist, he immediately adds in brackets, "the whole Roman Empire [the future

---

[53] *Oikoumene* is entry 3625 in the "Greek Dictionary of the New Testament" section of James Strong, *Strong's Exhaustive Concordance of the Bible*. 34th printing. Nashville: Abingdon Press, 1976.

[54] In his comment on Luke 2:1, Vincent defines *oikoumene* as follows: "Literally, *the inhabited (land)*. This phrase was originally used by the Greeks to denote the land inhabited by themselves, in contrast with barbarian countries; afterward, when the Greeks became subject to the Romans, *the entire Roman world*; still later, for *the whole inhabited world*" (emphasis in original). Marvin R. Vincent, *Word Studies in the New Testament*. *Volume I*. Originally published 1886. Peabody, Massachusetts: Hendrickson Publishers, reprinted 1985: 266. In Jesus' prophecy in Matthew 24, it seems most likely that *oikoumene* is used as "the entire Roman world," which further means his prophecy was fulfilled in the first century.

revived empire]."[55] However, it's much more probable that Jesus was simply referring to the Roman Empire of the first-century church.

According to many biblical passages, the Roman Empire of the first century *did* hear the gospel before A.D. 70. "These that have turned the world [*oikoumene*] upside down have come hither also," cried out the Thessalonians (Acts 17:6). Paul told the Roman church, "Your faith is spoken of *throughout the whole world*" (Romans 1:8), and wrote further of this triumphant witness elsewhere in his letters:

- ". . . according to my gospel, and the preaching of Jesus Christ, according to the revelation of the mystery, which . . . now is made manifest, and . . . *made known to all nations* for the obedience of faith" (Romans 16:25-26).
- ". . . be not moved away from the hope of the gospel, which ye have heard, and which was *preached to every creature* which is under heaven" (Colossians 1:23).
- "For the hope which is laid up for you in heaven, whereof ye heard before in the word of the truth of the gospel: which is come unto you, as it is in *all the world*, and bringeth forth fruit, as it doth also in you" (Colossians 1:5-6).
- "But I say, Have they not heard? Yes verily, their sound went into *all the earth*, and their words unto *the ends of the world* [*oikoumene*]" (Romans 10:18).
- And so on.

So it seems legitimate to interpret the prophecy of Jesus literally. The gospel would be preached to all the Roman Empire (all the *oikoumene* world), and then the end (of Jerusalem and the Temple) would come. Adam Clarke comments, "When this general publication of the Gospel shall have taken place, then a period shall be put to the whole Jewish economy, by the utter destruction of their city and temple."[56] This is what Jesus means when He says, "And then shall the end come."

In fact, this view helps explain the next few verses of Matthew 24:

[15] When ye therefore shall see the abomination of desolation, spoken of by Daniel the prophet, stand in the holy place (whoso readeth, let him understand),

---

[55] Kenneth Wuest, *The New Testament: An Expanded Translation*. Grand Rapids, Michigan: Eerdmans Publishing, 1961.

[56] Adam Clarke, *Commentary on Matthew*. In *Parallel Classic Commentary on the New Testament*. Edited by Mark Water. Chattanooga, Tennessee: AMG Publishers, 2004: 339.

[16] Then let them which be in Judea flee into the mountains:

[17] Let him which is on the housetop not come down to take anything out of his house:

[18] Neither let him which is in the field return back to take his clothes.

[19] And woe unto them that are with child, and to them that give suck in those days!

[20] But pray ye that your flight be not in the winter, neither on the Sabbath day:

[21] For then shall be great tribulation, such as was not since the beginning of the world to this time, no, nor ever shall be.

[22] And except those days should be shortened, there should no flesh be saved: but for the elect's sake those days shall be shortened.

Preterist: Jesus is specifically warning the people of Judea, the observant Jews who would keep the Sabbath day, that they would face "great tribulation" very soon. However, He also points out in verse 22 that some of the Jewish people would make it through those horrible days. The "abomination of desolation" is also explainable as a first-century event; in fact, the parallel to this passage in Luke's Gospel records Jesus as saying Jerusalem's "desolation" occurs when the city is "compassed with armies," probably a prediction of the siege of Titus in the year 70 (Luke 21:20).

Futurist: Look, the promise of the imminent coming of Christ is a great help in motivating Christians to witness to the unsaved world before the end comes. Given your description of a "first-century coming," what happens to that motivation in the present-day church?

Preterist: I don't think anything necessarily has to happen to our motivation. Why couldn't we have the same motivation the early church had: the motivation that people need salvation, that the unsaved should hear of God's redeeming love in Christ, and that our love constrains us to reach out?

Futurist: All right, but that's not my primary objection to your position, anyway. . . .

[*To be continued in the next chapter.*]

7. Matthew 24 (Part 2): What Does "Coming in the Clouds" Really Mean?

[The debate continues. . . .]

Futurist: Look, the promise of the imminent coming of Christ is a great help in motivating Christians to witness to the unsaved world before the end comes. Given your description of a "first-century coming," what happens to that motivation in the present-day church?

Preterist: I don't think anything necessarily has to happen to our motivation. Why couldn't we have the same motivation the early church had: the motivation that people need salvation, that the unsaved should hear of God's redeeming love in Christ, and that our love constrains us to reach out?

Futurist: All right, but that's not my primary objection to your position, anyway. You've done an ingenious job of explaining away these prophetic truths, but . . .

Preterist: I'd rather think of it as "explaining" instead of "explaining away."

Futurist: At any rate, let me point out a much different linking together of these scriptures. The Christian church of today is preaching the gospel to all the world and will round out that task, "looking for and hastening the coming of the day of God" (2 Peter 3:12). At that (future) point, the end shall come and Jesus Christ shall return for his saints in the Rapture. After Jesus catches away his church, the "abomination of desolation" will then be set up by the Antichrist in the restored Temple as prophesied in the Book of Daniel, and a ferocious persecution of the Jews will ensue, during which many will flee into the wilderness areas of Israel. We find out elsewhere (not here in Matthew) that this "great tribulation" will last for seven years. After this, in the next few verses of Jesus' prophecy in Matthew 24, we see the next great event in God's prophetic timetable—the Second Coming of the Lord:

> [23] Then if any man shall say unto you, Lo, here is Christ, or there; believe it not.

[24] For there shall arise false Christs, and false prophets, and shall show great signs and wonders; insomuch that, if it were possible, they shall deceive the very elect.

[25] Behold, I have told you before.

[26] Wherefore if they shall say unto you, Behold, he is in the desert; go not forth: behold, he is in the secret chambers; believe it not.

[27] For as the lightning cometh out of the east, and shineth even unto the west; so shall also the coming of the Son of man be.

[28] For wheresoever the carcass is, there will the eagles be gathered together.

[29] Immediately after the tribulation of those days shall the sun be darkened, and the moon shall not give her light, and the stars shall fall from heaven, and the powers of the heavens shall be shaken:

[30] And then shall appear the sign of the Son of man in heaven: and then shall all the tribes of the earth mourn, and they shall see the Son of man coming in the clouds of heaven with power and great glory.

[31] And he shall send his angels with a great sound of a trumpet, and they shall gather together his elect from the four winds, from one end of heaven to the other.

[32] Now learn a parable of the fig tree; When his branch is yet tender, and putteth forth leaves, ye know that summer is nigh:

[33] So likewise ye, when ye shall see all these things, know that it is near, even at the doors.

[34] Verily I say unto you, This generation shall not pass, till all these things be fulfilled.

[35] Heaven and earth shall pass away, but my words shall not pass away.

[36] But of that day and hour knoweth no man, no, not the angels of heaven, but my Father only.

Preterist: Wouldn't this be a "Third Coming" according to your view, since Jesus already came back previously in the Rapture?

Futurist: No. In the Rapture (which I think of as the "first stage" of the Second Coming), Jesus comes for his church, but does not actually return "to" the earth.

Preterist: I think that's a semantic quibble (and wrong for other reasons to be discussed in a later chapter), but I'll let it pass.

Futurist: We also see in this passage another reason why I cannot accept your position on these prophecies. In verse 27, the return of Christ is described as "lightning." And especially look at verses 29-30, where Jesus describes the sun as darkened, the moon not giving light, the stars falling from heaven, the powers of the heavens shaken, and especially all the earth seeing the Son of man coming in the clouds of heaven with great glory. I take these words as a literal description of end-time events according to Jesus Himself—and none of them has happened yet. Have these atmospheric signs occurred yet? Did "all the tribes of the earth mourn" and "see" the coming of Jesus "in the clouds of heaven" at the destruction of Jerusalem? We must respond in the negative, to both of these questions. So we know that at least these events certainly did not happen in the first century. However, I imagine you'll now argue that they did.

Preterist: That's correct; I think they did occur. You see, Jesus is ministering in the tradition of the Hebrew prophets, who often used the exact same imagery that Jesus uses here to describe God's judgment on a civilization or on a specific city or area. For example, the prophets often described the Lord as "coming in the clouds" to deal with his enemies[57]:

- In Isaiah: "The burden of Egypt. Behold, the Lord rideth *upon a swift cloud*, and shall come into Egypt: and the idols of Egypt shall be moved at his presence, and the heart of Egypt shall melt in the midst of it" (19:1).

- In Jeremiah: "Behold, *He shall come up as clouds*, and his chariots shall be as a whirlwind. . . . O Jerusalem, wash thine heart from wickedness, that thou mayest be saved" (4:13-14).

- In Ezekiel: "For the day is near, even the day of the Lord is near, *a cloudy day*; it shall be the time of the heathen. . . . At Tehaphnehes also *the day shall be darkened*, when I shall break there the yokes of Egypt: and the pomp of her strength shall cease in her: as for her, *a cloud* shall cover her. . . . Thus will I execute judgments in Egypt: and they shall know that I am the Lord" (30:3, 18-19).

- In Nahum: "God is jealous, and the Lord revengeth; the Lord revengeth, and is furious; the Lord will take vengeance on his adversaries, and He reserveth wrath for his enemies. The Lord is slow to anger, and great in power, and will not at all acquit the wicked: the Lord hath his way in the whirlwind and in the storm, and *the clouds are the dust of his feet*" (1:2-3).

---

[57] The following examples are taken from Larry T. Smith, *The Coming of the Lord, the Last Days, and the End of the World*: 14-15.

According to the *Dictionary of Biblical Imagery*, "Clouds serve as God's war chariot in the imagination of the Old Testament poets and prophets. . . . One of the most pervasive images of Christ's return is as one who rides his cloud chariot into battle."[58]

So when Jesus says that the tribes of the earth "shall see the Son of man coming in the clouds of heaven with power and great glory," He means the nations will witness the stunning destruction of Jerusalem in A.D. 70, when the Lord comes in the clouds for judgment. Jesus is not talking like a television weather reporter predicting some rather odd conditions, but He *is* talking like Isaiah, Jeremiah, Ezekiel, and Nahum—like a biblical prophet, in other words.

Futurist: So you only think of Jesus' words as "imagery" rather than as reality?

Preterist: Your "imagery/reality" distinction is a false dilemma. "Imagery is not meant to be taken literally, but it *is* meant to be taken seriously."[59] Jesus is using a serious image, an image of coming destruction and ruin. He's not talking about a cloudy day; He's talking about events that are really going to occur in the lives of his first-century hearers.

In fact, understanding this figure of speech also enables us to understand something from very early on in the Book of Revelation: "Behold, He cometh with clouds; and every eye shall see Him, and they also which pierced Him: and all kindreds of the earth shall wail because of Him. Even so, Amen" (Revelation 1:7). Jesus' returning in judgment against Jerusalem would have been described in biblical prophecy as coming "with clouds." Further, since this refers to a first-century return, some would still be alive from the generation "which pierced Him"; if this were not referring to a first-century return in judgment, none of those who helped crucify Him would be there to "see Him," as is indicated. Again, we should keep in mind the dating of the Book of Revelation—just before the destruction of A.D. 70.[60]

The disturbances of the sun, moon, and stars also are common images found in the prophets. "In the prophetic language, great commotions upon

---

[58] "Cloud," from the *Dictionary of Biblical Imagery*. Edited by L. Ryken, J.C. Wilhoit, and T. Longman III. Downers Grove, Illinois: InterVarsity Press, 1998: 157.

[59] Peter Kreeft and Ronald K. Tacelli, *Handbook of Christian Apologetics*. Downers Grove, Illinois: InterVarsity Press, 1994: 308. Emphasis in original.

[60] For the discussion of Revelation's date of composition, see Chapter 4, "Why Should We Prefer the Preterist View?" and especially Chapter 12, "Fifteen More Questions about Revelation."

earth are often represented under the notion of commotions and changes in the heavens"[61]:

- The fall of Babylon is represented by the stars and constellations of heaven withdrawing their light, and the sun and moon being darkened (Isaiah 13:9-10).
- The destruction of Egypt is represented by the heaven being covered, the sun enveloped with a cloud, and the moon withholding her light (Ezekiel 32:7-8).
- The coming of the Assyrians into Israel is represented by the sun going down at noon and darkness on a clear day (Amos 8:9).
- The destruction of the Jews by Antiochus Epiphanes is represented by casting down some of the host of heaven, and the stars to the ground (Daniel 8:10).
- And this very destruction of Jerusalem is represented by the prophet Joel (Joel 2:30-31) by showing wonders in heaven and in earth—darkening the sun, and turning the moon into blood.

"This general mode of describing these judgments leaves no room to doubt the propriety of its application in the present case [i.e., in Matthew 24]."[62] The Lord coming in the clouds, the sun, moon, and stars being darkened, the powers of the heavens being shaken—all this took place at the Lord's coming in judgment upon Jerusalem, in A.D. 70.

Futurist: Here we see a good example of what John Walvoord describes in his commentary on the Book of Revelation: "The Preterist view, in general, tends to destroy any future significance of [biblical prophecy], which becomes a literary curiosity with little prophetic meaning."[63] What meaning do Jesus' words have for believers today if, as you say, these prophecies have been fulfilled for two millennia already?

Preterist: I don't think Walvoord's comment is necessarily accurate. Look at Isaiah 53, for example, the prophecy of the Suffering Messiah: Most Christians think that particular prophecy has already been fulfilled in the sacrificial crucifixion of Christ. However, just because Isaiah's words are already fulfilled does not take away any part of their significance for us, since they reveal Jesus more fully to us as our great Redeemer. Likewise, even if Jesus' prophetic words in Matthew 24 have already been fulfilled,

---

[61] This and the following scriptural examples are taken from Adam Clarke, *Commentary on Matthew*. In *Parallel Classic Commentary on the New Testament*: 343.

[62] Ibid., p. 343.

[63] John F. Walvoord, *The Revelation of Jesus Christ: A Commentary*. Chicago: Moody Press, 1966: 18.

they still have significance for us. They reveal Jesus to us even more fully as the Lord of all the earth and the great Judge of the nations.

[*To be concluded in the next chapter. . . .*]

8. Matthew 24 (Part 3): Who Are "Left Behind"?

[The debate continues for one more chapter. . . .]

Futurist: Here we see a good example of what John Walvoord describes in his commentary on the Book of Revelation: "The Preterist view, in general, tends to destroy any future significance of [biblical prophecy], which becomes a literary curiosity with little prophetic meaning."[64] What meaning do Jesus' words have for believers today if, as you say, these prophecies have been fulfilled for two millennia already?

Preterist: I don't think Walvoord's comment is necessarily accurate. Look at Isaiah 53, for example, the prophecy of the Suffering Messiah: Most Christians think that particular prophecy has already been fulfilled in the sacrificial crucifixion of Christ. However, just because Isaiah's words are already fulfilled does not take away any part of their significance for us, since they reveal Jesus more fully to us as our great Redeemer. Likewise, even if Jesus' prophetic words in Matthew 24 have already been fulfilled, they still have significance for us. They reveal Jesus to us even more fully as the Lord of all the earth and the great Judge of the nations.

Let's look at one more section of Matthew 24, the passage dealing specifically with those who are "left behind":

[37] But as the days of Noah were, so shall also the coming of the Son of man be.

[38] For as in the days that were before the flood they were eating and drinking, marrying and giving in marriage, until the day that Noah entered into the ark,

[39] And knew not until the flood came, and took them all away; so shall also the coming of the Son of man be.

[40] Then shall two be in the field; the one shall be taken, and the other left.

---

[64] John F. Walvoord, *The Revelation of Jesus Christ: A Commentary.* Chicago: Moody Press, 1966: 18.

[41] Two women shall be grinding at the mill; the one shall be taken, and the other left.

[42] Watch therefore: for ye know not what hour your Lord doth come.

Futurist: Yes, this is a wonderful passage. At this point Jesus reiterates his central message: Be on the alert at all times, for the catching away of the church could occur at any moment, and you don't want to be one of those "left behind."

Preterist: Well, here at least is one thing on which we can agree: Christians should always be on the alert for the moving of God in their lives and circumstances, for we don't want to be "left behind" in his purposes and dealings. However, in context, this "left behind" passage, contrary to the series of novels by that name, is not referring to a catching away of the Church.

This seems obvious even from a cursory reading of the text. Jesus says that his coming will occur "as in the days of Noah"; He further points out that the people judged by God in the days of Noah "knew not until the flood came, and took them all away." In other words, it is *the people who are judged* who are "taken away" to judgment and death, and the righteous Noah and his family who are "left behind" on the earth—those "left behind" are spared from judgment!

Of course, this parallels the pattern established in the Old Testament prophets. For example, in the Babylonian Captivity of Israel's southern kingdom, those judged by God are taken away to captivity in Babylon, while those spared this fate are "left behind" in the land of Judah (Jeremiah 39:9-10):

> Then Nebuzaradan the captain of the guard carried away captive into Babylon the remnant of the people that remained in the city, and those that surrendered to him, with the rest of the people that remained. But Nebuzaradan left of the poor of the people, which had nothing, in the land of Judah, and gave them vineyards and fields at the same time.

In Jesus' parallel prophecy in Luke's Gospel, when He refers to those who "shall be taken," the disciples immediately ask a natural question: "Where, Lord?"—i.e., "Where will those taken away be taken?" Jesus replies, "Wheresoever the body is, thither will the eagles be gathered together" (Luke 17:37). This is probably a reference to the armies of Rome, whose standard was the Roman eagle, surrounding the dead body of Jerusalem like vultures at a kill. But however one interprets this verse, it certainly cannot be interpreted as the joyous, celebratory occasion of the Church being caught up to reign with Christ eternally.

So, thanks to the recent series of "Left Behind" novels, here we have the most famous passage in the New Testament regarding the Rapture of the Church—and it doesn't really refer to the Rapture at all!

Futurist: Before you confuse the issue any further, let me offer an alternate interpretation and an objection. First, when Jesus refers to those "left behind" and those "taken away"—even in the case of Noah and his world—He does not mean the judged were "taken away" to judgment and Noah and his family were "left behind" to be spared. He means Noah was "taken away" *from* judgment, and the rest were "left behind" *to face* judgment. So the "Left Behind" novels are indeed titled entirely appropriately. Those not going in the Rapture will be "left behind" to face tribulation.

Preterist: But Jesus Himself said of those destroyed in judgment that the flood "took them all away." He is not referring to Noah and his family, is he?

Futurist: Well, at any rate, that's the alternate interpretation. Here's the objection: You say that Jesus' words here do not really refer to the Rapture of the Church at all even while you call his words "the most famous passage in the New Testament regarding the Rapture." But even that is an arguable point. What about Paul's words to the Thessalonians:

> For the Lord Himself shall descend from heaven with a shout, with the voice of the archangel, and with the trump of God: and the dead in Christ shall rise first: then we which are alive and remain shall be caught up together with them in the clouds, to meet the Lord in the air: and so shall we ever be with the Lord. (1 Thes. 4:16-17)

Even if Jesus' prophecy in Matthew's Gospel does not completely spell out all end-time events, there are other passages in the New Testament (such as this one) that you cannot explain away with a first-century fulfillment. These verses clearly describe a yet-future catching away of the church.

Preterist: I still don't think so. In order to rightly understand Paul's words here in First Thessalonians, you have to understand first of all that Paul is not writing of the Rapture.

Futurist: What? How else can you explain the meaning of believers being "caught up together" in the clouds "to meet the Lord in the air," except as referring to the Rapture? Now you are just being ridiculous.

Preterist: Not at all. In fact, Paul is using an image that would have been rather familiar to his first-century readers. . . .

(But we will have to deal with this issue in the next chapter.)

9. But Paul Writes About the Rapture, Doesn't He?

"Behold, I show you a mystery: We shall not all sleep, but we shall all be changed" (1 Corinthians 15:51).

In the dramatized debate of the last chapter, we closed with one of the most well-known passages used by futurists to support belief in the Rapture. Not coincidentally, this passage is found in one of Paul's epistles —"not coincidentally" because the argument is often made that even though Jesus might not have spoken clearly and unambiguously about the Rapture, the full revelation of the doctrine *is* found unambiguously spelled out in Paul's writings. In this chapter, we will examine two selections from Paul's epistles that are used to bolster this argument. The first selection, previously quoted, is found in Paul's First Epistle to the Thessalonians:

> But I would not have you to be ignorant, brethren, concerning them which are asleep, that ye sorrow not, even as others which have no hope. For if we believe that Jesus died and rose again, even so them also which sleep in Jesus will God bring with him. For this we say unto you by the word of the Lord, that we which are alive and remain unto the coming of the Lord shall not prevent [or "precede"] them which are asleep.

The first important point to note about this passage is that Paul is primarily writing regarding concerns about the great resurrection of the dead. (These concerns will also be addressed in the selection from First Corinthians, to be examined next.) Early Christians wondered: What happens to those who have died? Specifically, if Christ were to return in the first century, would He return only for those who were still alive? Would those who had already died be left out of the accounting of the elect? In what manner would the Second Coming occur if some involved had died and some were still alive? Would those living have a better or favored status than those in the grave? Have we lost hope entirely for those who die before the Lord's coming? "There seems to have been a rumor in Thessalonica that the dead Christians had lost out on any chance of a physical resurrection."[65] Paul answers these questions by noting that those who had died were *already with* the Lord; God would bring them "with" Christ at his Return. Those alive at that time would have no favored or privileged standing because of their still-living condition; they would not "precede" in any way those who had died. Therefore, Christians need not sorrow as those "which have no hope":

> For the Lord Himself shall descend from heaven with a shout, with the voice of the archangel, and with the trump of God: and the dead in Christ shall rise first: then we which are alive and remain shall be caught up together with them in the clouds, to meet the Lord in the air: and so shall we ever be with the Lord. (1 Thes. 4:13-17)

For many futurists, this is the most vivid and compelling biblical picture of the "Rapture," in which living believers are to be "caught up together . . . in the clouds." The Lord shouts "with the voice of the archangel" and with the sound of a trumpet blast; the dead in Christ rise out of their graves; we who are alive are instantaneously transformed and rise into the clouds, "to meet the Lord in the air"; and thus we enter into eternity "with the Lord." It certainly seems a plausible reading of the passage. But is it accurate?

A second important point to note here is that in his description of this crucial event in human and divine history and relations, Paul is echoing an Old Testament passage relating yet another crucial event in human and divine history and relations. In the book of Exodus, Moses leads the Israelites out of Egypt and into the area of Mount Sinai. The Lord Himself then speaks to Moses, "Ye have seen what I did unto the Egyptians, and how I bare you on eagles' wings and brought you unto myself. Now therefore, if ye will obey my voice indeed, and keep my covenant, then ye shall be a peculiar treasure unto me above all people" (19:4-5). Moses relays these words to the other Israelites, who pledge to obey God in all He commands. The Lord then tells Moses, "Lo, I come to thee in a thick cloud. . . . [On] the third day the Lord will come down in the sight of all the people upon Mount Sinai" (9-11). Again, Moses passes along these words and instructs the people to be prepared for the divine manifestation and visitation:

> And it came to pass on the third day in the morning, that there were thunders and lightnings, and a thick cloud upon the mount, and the voice of the trumpet exceeding loud; so that all the people

---

[65] David B. Currie. *Rapture: The End-Times Error That Leaves the Bible Behind.* Manchester, New Hampshire: Sophia Institute Press, 2003: 204.

that were in the camp trembled. And Moses brought forth the people out of the camp to meet with God; and they stood at the nether part of the mount. And Mount Sinai was altogether on a smoke, because the Lord descended upon it in fire: and the smoke thereof ascended as the smoke of a furnace, and the whole mount quaked greatly. And when the voice of the trumpet sounded long, and waxed louder and louder, Moses spake, and God answered him by a voice. And the Lord came down upon Mount Sinai, on the top of the mount: and the Lord called Moses up to the top of the mount; and Moses went up. (Exodus 19:16-20)

After this awesome event, Moses returns down from the mountain to give the people the Decalogue, the great Ten Commandments by which they were to live. "And all the people saw the thunderings, and the lightnings, and the noise of the trumpet, and the mountain smoking: and when the people saw it, they removed [moved away] and stood afar off" (20:18).

Some parallels become obvious as we examine these passages together:

- A great "turning-point" event occurs—in the one case, we see the giving of the Ten Commandments to Moses, to establish the Israelites in a special relationship with the Lord, that they might live unto Him in the reign of God's Law; in the other case related by Paul, we see the Coming of the Lord Himself to unite all believers eternally, that they might live unto Him forever in his reign upon the Earth.

- Both events involve great noise: the voice of the archangel, the voice of God, thunder, lightning, earthquakes, and so on.

- Even more specifically, both events involve the noise of a trumpet blast: in the one case, the "trump of God" and in the other a "trumpet exceeding loud" that "sounded long, and waxed louder and louder": "the sound of a trumpet, and the voice of words," as the New Testament describes it (Hebrews 12:19).

- Both events involve the Lord's coming down in a cloud to meet with his people: "Lo, I come to thee in a thick cloud," as God tells Moses. As Moses goes up to meet with God, the following occurs: "And it came to pass on the third day in the morning, that there were thunders and lightnings, and a thick cloud upon the mount." Likewise Paul writes, "The Lord Himself shall descend from heaven" and "we which are alive and remain shall be caught up together with them in the clouds."

We see many parallels between these events, but what constitutes their relationship? It is just this: After Moses, the man of God, goes up to meet with the Lord in the clouds on the mountain, he returns back down to the people of God, to inaugurate a new type of rule, a new society under the rule of God's Law. Note particularly that Moses *goes up in order immediately to come back down*. Likewise, *after the people of God go up* to meet with the Lord in the clouds of the heavens, *they will immediately return back down with Him* to be the people of God in his new society, to inaugurate Christ's new rule on Earth. In other words, Paul in First Thessalonians simply does not present a picture of the Rapture taking people *away from* the earth, but rather a picture of the Second Coming of the Lord *to* the earth, a coming to Earth to establish his new reign, a kingdom under the rule of God's Word.

Other writers have made similar arguments with additional details. For example, David Currie points out, "Rapturists make a point of the fact that we will 'meet the Lord in the air'—the Lord who has come 'in the clouds.'" However, "The word St. Paul uses for meeting the Lord 'in the air' is *aer*, the Greek word for *atmosphere*. . . . When Christ returns to the earth's atmosphere, He has returned to earth. . . . We will meet Christ, but it will be at His second coming to earth. Any other use of the language stretches credibility."[66] Another author, Paul Thigpen, explains this meeting in terms of a custom known well to Greek and Roman society:

> As we have seen, the context of the 1 Thessalonians passage, with its references to the angel, the trumpet, and the clouds, shows that St. Paul is writing about the glorious public return of the Lord [not a secret and private Rapture]. The question that arises is this: What is the purpose of the faithful on earth being "caught up" in the glory of their descending Lord to meet Him as He arrives in triumph? The answer is simple when we recognize an ancient custom common in St. Paul's culture. State dignitaries and victorious military leaders of his time often made grand public visits to a city. Such an appearance was called a *parousia*, the same Greek term that St. Paul and other biblical writers often use to write about Christ's glorious arrival at the close of the age.[67]

This custom holds much similarity to the Roman *triumphus*, the triumphal procession made for an outstandingly victorious warrior and commander. Thigpen goes on:

> When the illustrious visitor approached a city with his entourage, he was often met by the citizens who wanted to go out to welcome him and then accompany him back into the city. It was a way for

---

[66] Currie, *Rapture*, p. 205.
[67] Paul Thigpen. *The Rapture Trap*. West Chester, Penn.: Ascension Press, 2001: 113.

the people to honor such a person's arrival and to take part in the celebration of his coming, [such as we see in] Jesus' triumphal entry into Jerusalem on the day we remember as Passion (or Palm) Sunday. . . . When we find that the Greek word translated here as "meet" or "meeting" (*apantesis*) is the same term that was used for the gathering of citizens to meet the approaching celebrity, the passage makes perfect sense. Those who are still alive on earth when Jesus returns, gathered together from the ends of the earth by the angels, will have a great privilege: They will be caught up in His clouds of glory to meet the approaching "King of kings and Lord of lords" (1 Timothy 6:15) and to join the saints whose souls have already experienced the rewards of living with Him in heaven. Then they will accompany Him as He enters the world in triumph.[68]

This use of *apantesis* or "meeting" is corroborated by many other commentaries and reference works. For example, James Strong writes of *apantesis*: "Used in the papyri of a newly arriving magistrate, it seems that the special idea of the word was the official welcome of a newly arrived dignitary" (*Dictionary of Bible Words*); the same wording is used by William Moulton and W.E. Vine (*Vine's Expository Dictionary*); and James Moffatt writes of the use of *apantesis* in 1 Thessalonians 4, "Plainly, however, the saints do not rise at once to heaven, but return with the Lord to the scene of his final manifestation on earth" (*Expositor's Greek Testament*). Moffatt also points out that this non-Rapture reading was the interpretation favored by Chrysostom, Augustine, and others.

We should therefore consider carefully that belief in this prophetic passage of Scripture from Thessalonians does not necessarily entail belief in the Rapture, the time of tribulation, the rise of an Antichrist, the final battle of Armageddon, nor any other futurist teachings. It entails merely belief in what the Creeds have always stated: "He shall come again with glory, to judge the living and the dead." Such a wonderful prophecy, when rightly understood, holds great promise—and zero panic.

Earlier I wrote that we would examine two selections from Paul's epistles that are used to bolster the futurist position; let us now therefore turn to the second passage, from First Corinthians. Again, we should first note that Paul is writing to believers with concerns about the resurrection of the dead:

Now if Christ be preached that he rose from the dead, how say some among you that there is no resurrection of the dead? But if

---

[68] Ibid., pp. 113-14.

there be no resurrection of the dead, then is Christ not risen: And if Christ be not risen, then is our preaching vain, and your faith is also vain. Yea, and we are found false witnesses of God; because we have testified of God that he raised up Christ: whom he raised not up, if so be that the dead rise not. For if the dead rise not, then is not Christ raised: And if Christ be not raised, your faith is vain; ye are yet in your sins. Then they also which are fallen asleep in Christ are perished. If in this life only we have hope in Christ, we are of all men most miserable. But now is Christ risen from the dead, and become the first fruits of them that slept. For since by man came death, by man came also the resurrection of the dead. For as in Adam all die, even so in Christ shall all be made alive. But every man in his own order: Christ the first fruits; afterward they that are Christ's at his coming. (1 Cor. 15:12-23)

The sequence of Paul's logic goes as follows: If there is no such thing as the resurrection of the dead, it seems that would also apply to Christ, Who would therefore not be risen. However, since we know that Christ is risen, it would then follow that there is in fact a resurrection. Christ's resurrection thus may be seen as the type or first fruits of the future resurrection of *all* believers who have died in Him; this resurrection of believers will take place "at his coming."

The next few verses in this passage are crucial:

Then cometh the end, when he shall have delivered up the kingdom to God, even the Father; when he shall have put down all rule and all authority and power. For he must reign, till he hath put all enemies under his feet. The last enemy that shall be destroyed is death. (24-26)

According to futurists, after the Rapture there is an extended period of time beginning with the seven-year Tribulation, the climactic Battle of Armageddon, and then a thousand-year reign of peace known as the Millennium. All of this takes place *before* the final resurrection and judgment, in which death is finally destroyed. However, how can this be? In the case of Christian believers taken in the Rapture, it would seem that death is not the *last* enemy destroyed, but actually among the *first*. How can this belief be squared with Paul's words here?

Is it not rather much simpler to take Paul's words as written? The great Resurrection of the Dead occurs at Christ's coming (vs. 23); this would be the Second Coming, not the hypothetical Rapture. The end of this age arrives, in which the Kingdom of Christ is delivered up to God the Father. And death, the great enemy holding humankind in captivity and fear, is defeated by the general resurrection of which Christ's resurrection is the first fruit and prime exemplar.

"But some will say," as Paul continues to debate, "How are the dead raised up? And with what body do they come?" (vs. 35). The argument moves into an extended discussion of the nature of the new human body in the resurrection. Throughout this passage, it is important to keep in mind that the Corinthians are troubled by questions over the nature of the resurrection, and Paul is addressing their anxiety. One might paraphrase their position as follows: "Our loved ones have died a physical death. Yes, we believe that spiritually they are still living in the presence of the Lord, but what does that mean for us? Should the coming of the Lord take place, will it affect only our bodies (we who are still alive), or will it also affect the bodies of those who have died? How so? What is the nature of this resurrection of the dead of which you speak?" Paul describes the nature of the bodies of those resurrected, using examples such as a lowly seed being buried in the earth before rising as a glorious plant, and arrives at his conclusion of this discussion:

> Behold, I show you a mystery; We shall not all sleep, but we shall all be changed, in a moment, in the twinkling of an eye, at the last trump: for the trumpet shall sound, and the dead shall be raised incorruptible, and we shall be changed. For this corruptible must put on incorruption, and this mortal must put on immortality. So when this corruptible shall have put on incorruption, and this mortal shall have put on immortality, then shall be brought to pass the saying that is written, Death is swallowed up in victory. O death, where is thy sting? O grave, where is thy victory? The sting of death is sin; and the strength of sin is the law. But thanks be to God, which giveth us the victory through our Lord Jesus Christ. Therefore, my beloved brethren, be ye steadfast, unmovable, always abounding in the work of the Lord, forasmuch as ye know that your labor is not in vain in the Lord. (15:51-58)

According to futurists, this change, this great transformation, this magnificent defeat of death itself, will occur "in the twinkling of an eye" (vs. 52) at the Rapture. But how can this Rapture-oriented position be correct when the very next words after "in the twinkling of an eye" are "at the last trump"?

Remember once again, for futurists there is a rather long sequence of events involving many, many trumpet blasts (as spelled out in the Book of Revelation[69]) that must transpire *after* the Rapture occurs. Consequently, how could this sounding of the trumpet be the *final* trumpet?—that is, unless it is the very same trumpet we have encountered before, in the passage from First Thessalonians: the trumpet signaling the Second Coming, the Resurrection from the Dead, and the Final Judgment. In fact, we have encountered that same trumpet even earlier in our biblical reading, in the words of Jesus Himself:

> We have heard about that trumpet already. Recall the words of Jesus: "They will see the Son of Man coming on the clouds of heaven with power and great glory; and He will send out His angels with a loud trumpet call, and they will gather His elect from the four winds, from one end of heaven to the other" (Matthew 24:30-31). St. Paul is clearly describing the same event Jesus described. The Son appears in clouds of brilliant glory, the trumpet sounds, and the angels do His bidding to gather His people for resurrection and judgment.[70]

The discussion of this passage probably could be concluded at this point. Both of the prime examples of "Rapture teaching" to be found in Paul (in 1 Thessalonians 4 and 1 Corinthians 15) have already been shown to refer to Christ's Second Coming and the Resurrection of the Dead, not to a Rapture at all. However, I would like to bring up one more point we may glean from Paul's words, regarding the nature of the resurrection.

Paul writes that at this Second Coming of the Lord "we shall not all sleep, but we shall all be changed" (vs. 51). The Greek word for "all" in both cases is *pantes*, derived from *pas*, which is almost always simply translated as "all." Therefore, "we shall not all sleep" is usually taken as meaning "Not all of us will die" (i.e., some of us will be taken in the Rapture instead of dying). However, *pantes* is closely related to *pantos* (also derived from *pas*), which means "altogether, in every way, completely." Given Paul's extended argument concerning the resurrection all the way through the entire chapter, it strikes me as making much more sense to read it in that way: "We shall not altogether, in every way, completely sleep, but we shall altogether, in every way, completely be changed." He is reassuring the anxious Corinthians: "Yes, your loved ones have died; however, they did not altogether, in every way, completely (spirit, soul, and body) die, but only in *body*. On the other hand, listen to this: We shall altogether, in every way, completely (spirit, soul, *and body*) be changed at the Great Resurrection, the Coming of the Lord. We will never *completely* die, and your loved ones

---

[69] The seven trumpets of Revelation will be discussed in the next two chapters.

[70] Thigpen, *The Rapture Trap*, p. 110.

have not *completely* died—but we will all, both living and dead, be *completely* changed in the Resurrection."

What an encouragement! How nicely such a statement concludes Paul's reassuring words to the Church; in fact, what a good example of "prophecy without panic." "Therefore," as Paul says, "be ye steadfast, unmovable, always abounding in the work of the Lord, forasmuch as ye know that your labor is not in vain in the Lord" (vs. 58). Thanks to God for his blessed prophetic word, giving us strength for our ongoing labors.

10. So—Briefly—What Is the Book of Revelation All About?

"And though St. John saw many strange monsters in his vision, he saw no creature so wild as one of his own commentators."[71]

In an earlier chapter, I mentioned that many people asking the question "Do you think we are living in the end times?" do not understand what the answer "Yes" might mean, not out of lack of intelligence, but because they have asked the question with certain preconceptions in mind. The same problem definitely crops up as we approach the Book of Revelation. One's interpretation of what exactly is going on in that book is influenced, and possibly even determined, by one's preconceived method of reading it. What should we have in mind as we begin looking through its pages?

Think of this as an analogy: The earliest known piece of writing in Old English is the epic poem *Beowulf*, anonymously written in about the year A.D. 800 but based on an older oral tale. The poem tells the story of the Scandinavian hero Beowulf and his encounters with the monsters Grendel, Grendel's mother (who is even more powerful and ferocious than her son), and a great dragon. If you have never read this work, you will want to do so someday soon, and so I will not give away anything that happens. My point is simply this: When we read *Beowulf*, we understand that it is an epic poem and work of fiction. Now suppose someone read it and immediately rushed off to Northern Europe to begin searching for the bones of the slain dragon, muttering to himself, "I *knew* it; I always *knew* there were real dragons." We would say that this reader took the poem too literally and so missed the fictional point.

Or suppose someone thought of the work as *entirely* fictional; while at a party, a friend brings up a recent vacation in Denmark and Sweden, and mentions enjoying a museum of Viking relics. This second reader yawns and says, "I don't really bother much with fairy tales and fantasy; you know, Denmark, Sweden, Vikings, and all that. I got enough of that out of

---

[71] G.K. Chesterton. *Orthodoxy* [1908]. From *Heretics/Orthodoxy* in the *Nelson's Royal Classics* series. Nashville: Thomas Nelson, 2000: 178.

Beowulf." We would say this reader did not rightly appreciate the history and culture serving as the background and undergirding of the epic. In both cases, the readers missed the full significance of the work because of their own preconceptions brought with them to the reading: In the first case, the reader thought he was reading a work of history rather than fiction; in the second case, the reader thought she was reading a work of complete fantasy, unrelated to anything or anyone actually seen in history.

In the same way, our preconceptions brought to Revelation certainly deeply affect our understanding of it. Is it history? What did it mean to the early Christian church? Is it a prophecy of our own future, with no connection to the early church? Its apocalyptic imagery is so striking and bizarre, one might even wonder: Is it even supposed to make sense at all, or is it a series of images designed to make us *feel* a certain way? Just as importantly: In what style is it written? Are we supposed to read it in a straightforward, chronological, linear fashion like a novel? Or is it a sort of "loop," presenting the same basic ideas over and over from a different angle?

Let us begin with these last two questions. Futurists typically read the Book of Revelation as one would read a novel—not in the sense of thinking of it as fiction, but in the sense of reading it in a chronological and linear fashion. Chapter 17, for example, comes later than Chapter 14, and so also is seen by futurists as coming later in time in its prophetic fulfillment; Chapter 14 comes later than Chapter 10, which is later than Chapter 8; the Seven Plagues come after the Seven Trumpets, which come after the Seven Seals; and so on. In this view, the book opens with messages to churches active in the author's day, but quickly (in Chapter 4) switches to an exposition of events yet to come in our future, presented sequentially according to the linear manner in which they are to occur. In other words, like a novel, Revelation has a beginning, a middle, and an ending, and the events described therein happen in that order. Therefore, for futurists the events described in Revelation have little or nothing to do with the early Christians and the special problems they were facing; rather, the images and symbols used in the book are to be interpreted as applying to our own future and what is to come upon the earth historically and literally, in a sequential order according to the book's sequential chapters. In this view, after the opening three chapters, the rest of Revelation is still in our future.

But what happens if we were to read the book in the second style described? That is, what if Revelation is something more like a "loop," presenting the same basic ideas over and over from a different angle—like a photographer in an airplane circling a battlefield, taking photo after photo of the same events, but from different perspectives? As we will see, this reading would certainly lend itself more readily to the preterist interpretation; it would also mean that the book would have had much more meaning and impact for the first generation of Christians hearing and reading it, since its prophetic significance would not have been "held back" for our own generation.

Further, if we were to think of the book in this way, a repetitive arrangement of materials quickly leaps out. There are seven groups of seven items making up most of the content of Revelation, each group of items presenting different details as we read along. These seven groups may be charted as follows:

1. Seven churches are listed (in chapters 1-3)
2. Seven seals on a scroll (4-7)
3. Seven trumpets (8-11)
4. Seven thunders (10-14)
5. Seven plagues (15-17a)
   Seven heads on a beast, which represent both:
6. Seven mountains (Rome) AND
7. Seven rulers (also Rome) (chapters 17b-18)

The remaining final chapters of Revelation break out of this pattern in order to present a look at the ultimate victory of Christ, the triumphant future which comes after the traumatic events preceding. However, the main body of the book is made up of these seven cycles of seven events, one after another, throughout the first eighteen chapters.

Given the symbolic significance of the number seven as a time of "completion" (like the seven days of a week or the seven days of Creation), it seems more fitting to read these events not as a chronological or linear vision, like a novel or movie, but rather as different views of the exact same set of events, each view complete in itself. In other words, each cycle of seven may be read as a different "snapshot," from a different angle, of the same events seen by John as he "circles around" the vision. In this sense, therefore, most of Revelation's fulfillment would have been in the near future of the early Christians as they read it, but not in *our* future, as a futurist would maintain, except for perhaps the last few chapters.

Let us see if this sense of reading Revelation as a "loop" of seven repetitions holds up, by examining these seven "snapshots" more closely while also taking a quick tour of the Book of Revelation itself.

11. Seven "Snapshots" of Revelation

"The number 'seven' is the favorite number of Revelation."[72]

In the previous chapter, the idea was introduced that the Book of Revelation is written in a "cyclical" style, presenting the same basic ideas over and over from a different angle—like a photographer in an airplane circling a battlefield, taking photo after photo of the same events, but from different perspectives. These "snapshots" of the events taking place in Revelation are presented in seven cycles of seven (seven trumpets, seven seals of a scroll, seven plagues, and so on). In other words, each cycle of seven may be read as a different "snapshot," from a different angle, of the same events seen by John as he "circles around" the vision.

In this chapter, we will take an overall view of Revelation by going through these seven cycles or "snapshots" one by one. Although it will require additional reading, this chapter will be of most benefit if read along with the chapters of Revelation given for each "snapshot."

Snapshot # 1: Seven Churches (Chapters 1-3):

In the first three chapters of Revelation, after a brief introduction in which John presents himself as being in forced exile on the island of Patmos, he encounters the risen Christ in a powerful visionary experience. In his right hand Christ holds seven stars as He walks among seven candlesticks or lampstands; He explains, "The seven stars are the angels of the seven churches; and the seven candlesticks which thou sawest are the seven churches" (1:20). The word for "angels" can also mean "messengers"; these are either literally supernatural angels or figuratively the human ministers in the various churches. Christ then gives John messages to these seven churches, which are located in Asia Minor, just east of John's position on Patmos. We will not look at each message individually, but rather at a few highlights. For example, early on John says of Jesus, "Behold, He cometh with clouds; and every eye shall see Him, and they also which

---

[72] G.K. Beale and Sean M. McDonough. "Revelation." *Commentary on the New Testament Use of the Old Testament.* G.K. Beale and D.A. Carson, eds. Grand Rapids, Michigan: Baker Academic, 2007: 1081-1161, p. 1089.

pierced Him: and all kindreds of the earth shall wail because of Him. Even so, Amen" (1:7). The meaning of "coming in the clouds" for judgment has already been discussed[73] and so will not be re-explained here. However, it is noteworthy that Jesus repeatedly declares that his coming is "soon" and "near" (vss. 1-3) and that He would be coming "quickly" (2:16; 3:11), both here at the beginning and also at the end of the book (22:11-12, 20). Those who would see his coming would be "they also which pierced Him," i.e., the Romans and Jews of the first century.

Jesus also repeatedly points out that his soon coming will be a coming in judgment regarding various issues taking place in some of the churches listed.[74] This listing therefore should probably be seen as an examination of the literal, historical churches named and their own particular problems, even if these scriptures also hold warnings and admonishments for our own lives today. Further, we find that Jesus has this authority to judge and rule not only churches, but also nations, because this authority has been given to Him:

> And he that overcometh, and keepeth my works unto the end, to
> him will I give power over the nations: and he shall rule them with
> a rod of iron; as the vessels of a potter shall they be broken to
> shivers: even as I received of my Father. (Rev. 2:26-27)

In this paraphrase from Psalm 2, Jesus warns believers that the "end" is coming soon, in which nations shall be "broken to shivers" by "a rod of iron" which He "received" of the Father. Given our knowledge after the facts, we can see that the very first nation judged in such a manner—shattered to fragments by the rod of Christ's judgment—is Israel itself, first in A.D. 70 and later as the nation is dispersed and its homeland dissolved. The Roman Empire itself is the rod of iron used by Christ to accomplish his purpose of judgment against those who rejected Him; as Jesus had prophesied in an earlier parable, Israel is the "fig tree" not producing fruit for its Owner (God). In that parable, Jesus Himself is the man who ministers to the tree for a few years to try to bring life and fruitfulness to it; however, He prophesies that its destiny eventually will come to pass: "Thou [God] shalt cut it down" (Luke 13:6-9). After Israel as a whole rejects the ministry of Christ, its judgment by God follows within a generation; it is indeed "cut down."

Finally, as Jesus approaches the conclusion of his messages to the seven churches, He tells the church of Philadelphia, "Because thou hast kept the

---

[73] In Chapter 7, "What Does 'Coming in the Clouds' Really Mean?"
[74] For example, in 2:5; 2:16; 3:3; 3:10-11; and so on.

word of my patience, I also will keep thee from the hour of temptation [the time of trial], which shall come upon *all the world*" (3:10, emphasis added). If this time of judgment does indeed come upon all the world as we typically understand the word "world," it would seem the preterist interpretation is gravely undermined; that is, these verses would not refer to the first-century judgment of Israel, but to a global trial and time of judgment. However, the word for "world" that Jesus uses here in his warning to the Philadelphian church is not the more typical Greek *kosmos* (the ordered creation) or *aion* (age, eon). Rather, He uses *oikoumene*, which we have discussed in a previous chapter.[75] *Oikoumene* means "land" or "the inhabited terrene world." To be even more precise, *oikoumene* means "specifically the Roman Empire," according to Strong's *Concordance*.[76] This time of trial of which Christ speaks is predicted as coming upon all the land—specifically, that land under Roman control.

So the first cycle of seven events in Revelation, the messages to the seven churches, can be seen as a preliminary warning of the fate of Israel, especially of the coming siege and destruction of Jerusalem, in the war already taking place between the Romans and Israel. What about the next cycle of seven?

Snapshot # 2: Seven Seals on a Scroll (Chapters 4-7):

Something amazing happens to John at this point:

> After this I looked, and, behold, a door was opened in heaven: and the first voice which I heard was as it were of a trumpet talking with me; which said, Come up hither, and I will show thee things which must be hereafter. And immediately I was in the spirit. . . . (Revelation 4:1-2)

According to futurists, this event depicts the Rapture of the Church, with John representing all Christians who are caught up together. A voice like a trumpet commands, "Come up hither," and John is at once in the heavenly realms. In this futurist interpretation, the first three chapters of Revelation are in our past, but everything from Chapter 4 onward has not yet come to pass; it is still in our future, and begins with the Rapture.

However, this scene does not reveal a "catching away" into Heaven, but rather an "unveiling" or *apocalupsis*, a revelation. John sees into God's throne room and the workings of Heaven which are always around us

---

[75] In Chapter 6, "Matthew 24 (Part 1): When Did the Whole World Hear the Gospel?"

[76] *Oikoumene* is entry 3625 in the "Greek Dictionary of the New Testament" section of James Strong, *Strong's Exhaustive Concordance of the Bible*. 34th printing. Nashville: Abingdon Press, 1976.

whether or not we always see them, always behind the events of our lives and the history of our days. He is not caught away *physically*; the command to "Come up hither" refers to passing into the heightened sense and vision of the spiritual realm for the purposes of God's forthcoming revelation. As N.T. Wright explains:

> This is not, as some people have supposed, anything to do with God's people being snatched away to heaven to avoid awful events that are about to take place on earth. . . . The scene in the heavenly throne room is the present reality . . . not "the end of the world" as such, but those terrible events which were going to engulf the world and cause all the suffering for God's people about which the seven churches have just been so thoroughly warned.[77]

Consequently, we are about to enter into the second of the "seven cycles of seven." God has pressed the "reset button" in John's prophetic visions, and we are about to take another look at the soon-to-come catastrophe in Jerusalem.

A scroll is produced in Heaven sealed with seven seals; the only one found worthy to open it is "a Lamb as it had been slain" (5:6). It is Jesus Himself, therefore, who opens the seals and unleashes the judgment. The opening of the first four seals brings forth the famous "Four Horsemen of the Apocalypse," usually titled "Conquest, War, Famine, and Death" (Chapter 6). Conquest and War in this case represent the Jewish/Roman War of A.D. 66-73:

> With the breaking of the first seal, the progression of events leading to the destruction of Jerusalem (in A.D. 70) begins. Horses represent war. The first four seals, when broken, release horses with their riders, hence, warfare and its accompaniments.[78]

The immediate accompaniment to Conquest and War is Famine; historically, this famine occurs halfway through the war, in the five-month siege of Jerusalem in A.D. 70. In his *Ecclesiastical History*, Eusebius quotes from Josephus, the well-known Jewish historian of the first century, and gives numerous details of the extent of this horrendous famine:

> Necessity forced them to apply their teeth to every thing, and gathering what was no food, even for the filthiest of irrational animals, they devoured it, and did not abstain at last even from belts and shoes. They took off the hides from their shields and devoured them, and some used even the remnants of old straw as

---

[77] N.T. Wright. *Revelation for Everyone*. Louisville, Kentucky: Westminster John Knox Press, 2011: 43-44.

[78] Steve Gregg, *Revelation: Four Views*, p. 102.

food; others gathered the stubble, and sold a very small weight of it for four Attic drachms.

In conclusion, as Eusebius continues to quote Josephus, he relates the story of Maria, the daughter of Eleazar, who had taken refuge at Jerusalem during the war; he writes, "I would cheerfully pass by this occurrence, if I had not innumerable witnesses still living." In short, Maria kills, roasts, and eats her son during the siege: "Forthwith the whole city was filled with the dreadful crime, and every one . . . was struck with a horror as if it had been perpetrated by himself." Eusebius ends his quotation and concludes, "Such then was the vengeance that followed the guilt and impiety of the Jews against the Christ of God."[79] As Jesus Himself prophesied of this time, "And when ye shall see Jerusalem compassed with armies, then know that the desolation thereof is nigh. . . . For these be the days of vengeance. . . . But woe unto *them that are with child*, and to *them that give suck*, in those days! For there shall be great distress in the land, and wrath upon this people" (Luke 21:20-23, emphasis added). Even as He walks on his way to the Crucifixion, Jesus specifically warns the "daughters of Jerusalem" *and their children* of the coming horrors (Luke 23:28-31).

The remaining three seals are opened as well. John sees the martyrs who had been "slain for the Word of God, and for the testimony which they held" (6:9). Great heavenly disturbances again signify the coming of the judgment of God (6:12-17).[80] However, a "great multitude" is yet saved out of this time of distress; John gives the symbolic number as 144,000 (7:4-9). We gain better understanding of this number later in Revelation, when John describes the walls of the New Jerusalem (the Church) as having twelve gates with "the twelve tribes of the children of Israel" written on them, and twelve foundations under the wall with "the names of the twelve apostles of the Lamb" (21:12-14). The 144,000, therefore, are the redeemed Church—those from the Old Covenant (12 tribes) multiplied by those from the New Covenant (12 apostles) multiplied by 1,000, the number of perfection and finality.[81] They remain as a witness to the truth and faithfulness of God to his Word, both in judgment and in salvation.

---

[79] *Ecclesiastical History*, Book III, Chapter VI.

[80] The language of great heavenly disturbances has already been discussed in Chap. 4, "Why Should We Prefer the Preterist View?"

[81] These are listed by their twelve Jewish tribal names because both the Jewish patriarchs and the original Christian apostles were Jewish. John is writing primarily to Jews regarding their own immediate future and the future of their country and Temple; hence he uses Jewish imagery.

Futurists hold that these 144,000 are still to come in the future, being Jewish converts to Christianity who evangelize after the Rapture. However, this group is later described as "the first fruits unto God and to the Lamb" (14:4). It would seem that the "first fruits" would be the very *first* converts from among the Jewish people in the first century, not among the "last fruits" 2,000 years or more in the future. They are also described as "without fault before the throne of God" (14:5); in other words, this 144,000 is actually the Church as seen through the lens of the salvation of Christ, "a glorious church, not having spot, or wrinkle, or any such thing," which is "holy and without blemish" before the Lord (Ephesians 5:27). John himself bears witness of this; after he *hears* "the number of them which were sealed" (144,000), he *sees* them: "After this I beheld, and lo, a great multitude, which no man could number, of all nations, and kindreds, and people . . . clothed with white robes" (7:9). This is a wondrous vision of the Church of Christ itself, not of a mere 144,000, but of a great and innumerable multitude.

Thus we conclude that the series of seven seals is again a picture of the judgment coming against Israel and particularly Jerusalem by means of the Jewish/Roman War of the first century. Added to this picture, however, is a vision of salvation as well, the redemption of the immense and glorious Church. The seven seals present a "snapshot" of the same events as previously pictured, but from a different perspective and with different details added.

Snapshot # 3: Seven Trumpets (Chapters 8-11):

In his vision, John next sees seven angels who are given seven trumpets to blow consecutively. Again the judgments begin with a series of four, as with the Four Horsemen of Chapter 6. These judgments are reminiscent of the judgments against Egypt in the book of Exodus in their specific character, in that they encompass hail from the sky, blood (as in the Nile changing to blood), the destruction of vegetation, the death of many (as in the death of the firstborn), and the darkening of the sun. Evidently the reader is supposed to recall that the Israelites were protected and led out from Egypt even as the Egyptians were judged; likewise God protects and leads out his people in Revelation from the judgment coming against Jerusalem. It is ironic indeed that in Revelation the city of Jerusalem and Israel itself are now taking the place of Egypt as the recipient of God's series of judgments; Jerusalem is even named "Egypt" by John later in the book (11:8).

These judgments come about in part because of the prayers of the martyrs seen in Chapter 6 "under the altar"; these martyrs had cried out,

"How long, O Lord, holy and true, dost thou not judge and avenge our blood on them that dwell on the earth?" (6:9-10). This cry for justice is answered when another angel, standing at the altar, mixes these prayers with incense and with "fire of the altar" (8:3-5); the angel then casts this mixture "into the earth," and the judgments of the trumpets officially begin.

As four angels blow the first four trumpets, an interesting phenomenon occurs: We see the death and desolation of "a third" of many various parts of creation. One-third of trees are burned up (8:7); one-third of the sea becomes blood (8); one-third of sea creatures die, along with the destruction of one-third of ships on the sea (9); a great burning star falls upon one-third of the rivers, poisoning one-third of fresh waters (10-11); one-third of the sun is "smitten," along with one-third of the moon and stars (12). What might this "one-third" repetition reveal?

At the time of the siege of Jerusalem, from April through September of the year 70, many Jews had come to Jerusalem and its surrounding area for the Passover; they then became trapped within the city by the encircling army. Out of these, the Roman historian Tacitus says that 600,000 Jews died during the ensuing famine and warfare, while Josephus puts the number of deaths at 1.1 million, with 97,000 taken captive.[82] Both of these historians' numbers seem rather high. A more modest estimate would be around 300,000 deaths out of about a million Jews living in the city and environs (although other estimates put the number of resident Jews at closer to three million, which would tend to validate the 1.1 million figure given by Josephus as the number of casualties). The important point is that the horrendous toll of death is about one-third of all the Jews in the area—which is what the Apostle John is writing about in the previously quoted verses. In one respect, then, these first four trumpets are highly figurative, while in another respect they are highly specific and historical. They are figurative in the many unusual symbols of nature used to convey the magnitude of this catastrophe, but specific and historical in giving exactly the number (one-third) of Jewish deaths during the siege and afterwards.

What happens to the other two-thirds during this war? Keep in mind that the siege of Jerusalem runs for about five months, from mid-April to mid-September, A.D. 70. According to John's prophecy, those two-thirds left alive will be tormented throughout this time, but will not die:

> And the fifth angel sounded. . . . And he opened the bottomless
> pit; and there arose a smoke out of the pit, as the smoke of a great
> furnace. . . . And there came out of the smoke locusts upon the

---

[82] Josephus, *The Jewish War*, VI.420-ff.

earth: and unto them was given power, as the scorpions of the earth have power. And it was commanded them that they should not hurt the grass of the earth, neither any green thing, neither any tree; but only those men which have not the seal of God in their foreheads. And to them it was given that they should not kill them, but that they should be tormented five months. . . . And in those days shall men seek death, and shall not find it; and shall desire to die, and death shall flee from them. . . . And their power was to hurt men five months. And they had a king over them, which is the angel of the bottomless pit, whose name in the Hebrew tongue is Abaddon, but in the Greek tongue hath his name Apollyon. (9:1-6; 10-11)

Here we see a vivid portrayal of the people locked within Jerusalem, longing for death during the five months of starvation imposed by the siege. The additional details of the "locusts" and the "angel" or messenger named Apollyon refer to the Fifteenth Apollonian Legion under General Titus, the legion of Roman soldiers (along with three other legions) encircling the city.[83] As can be seen by their name, the legion was dedicated to the god Apollo; "Apollyon" is a play on words, as it refers obliquely to Apollo but is a direct rendering into Greek of the Hebrew *Abaddon* or "Destroyer." As locusts were considered sacred to Apollo, it seems fitting that these swarming insects which destroy harvests and hence food supplies should personify both the pains of famine and the swarming, destructive soldiers of the Apollonian legion. Once again the death of "the third part of men" is mentioned (9:15, 18).

Snapshot # 4: Seven Thunders (Chapters 10-14):

The seven thunders are introduced in Chapter 10, overlapping with the seventh trumpet of Chapter 11. John is told to measure the Temple: however, "The court which is without the temple leave out, and measure it not; for it is given unto the Gentiles: and the holy city shall they tread under foot forty and two months" (11:2). Forty-two months is three and one-half years; the siege of Jerusalem ends with the devastating Roman victory halfway through the seven-year Jewish/Roman War, and so the Gentile forces rushing in tread under foot both the Temple and Jerusalem itself, the "holy city," for the last three and one-half years of the conflict, as John predicts. Although General Titus had wanted the beautiful Temple

---

[83] The Fifteenth Apollonian Legion was also the group that had earlier (A.D. 67) captured the Jewish general Yosef ben Matityahu and his forces. Matityahu later became better known as a historian under his Roman name, Josephus.

preserved from harm, by the time his soldiers had fought their way to the Temple they were beyond restraint, and the Temple was burned. According to traditional accounts of the battle, the gold and silver in the Temple melted and ran into the cracks of the Temple's stones, where it cooled and solidified again. In order to get this gold and silver, the Romans pried apart these very stones, thus fulfilling Jesus' prophecy regarding the Temple: "There shall not be left here one stone upon another, that shall not be thrown down" (Matthew 24:2).

"Two witnesses" then arise; although their identity is difficult to determine, John does give some hints to their character and abilities. "Fire" comes out of their mouths and "devours their enemies" (11:5); they also have "power to shut heaven, that it rain not" (6). Both of these traits call to mind the prophet Elijah, who called for both a drought and the ending of the drought, and who also called down fire from heaven upon his enemies. Likewise, the "power over waters to turn them to blood, and to smite the earth with all plagues" (6) clearly signifies Moses and the plagues against Egypt. It is therefore likely that Moses and Elijah together represent the Law and the Prophets, both of which point forward to Christ; in fact, Moses and Elijah are the two who appear to Jesus and his disciples to strengthen Him for his Passion (Luke 9:30-31). The fire out of their mouths which "devours their enemies" is the fire of the proclamation of God's Word: "Is not My Word like as a fire?" (Jeremiah 23:29). However, these two witnesses to Christ are rejected and even killed in Jerusalem: "Their dead bodies shall lie in the street of the great city, which spiritually is called Sodom and Egypt, where also our Lord was crucified" (8). Although conquered and seemingly killed, these two witnesses, the Law and the Prophets, rise again victoriously as their witness to Christ is vindicated; the prophetic scriptures of the Jewish people endure triumphantly, as Jesus Himself predicted they would (Matthew 5:17-18). As if to emphasize this victory, the seventh trumpet sounds, leading to a great celebration in Heaven of Christ's victory: "The kingdoms of this world are become the kingdoms of our Lord and of his Christ; and He shall reign forever and ever" (11:15). Therefore, I take the most plausible explanation of the two witnesses and the events surrounding them to be as follows: The Jewish people's very own Law (represented by Moses) and Prophets (represented by Elijah) are rejected and yet continue to live on to this day, testifying to the triumphant Lord.

A woman appears in heaven "clothed with the sun" who gives birth to "a man child, who was to rule all nations with a rod of iron" (12:1-5); this child is then taken up to God in Heaven (the Ascension of Christ). The woman has a multiple significance: individually, she is Mary the mother of Jesus; collectively, she is both Israel (who brought forth the Messiah) and the Church of Christ. The image here is also similar to a Greek story which John's readers would have known, the story of Leto, a woman pregnant with Apollo and Artemis. The dragon Python seeks to kill Leto to prevent the births, but she is protected and gives birth to the twins, whereupon Apollo, her male child, slays the dragon. The parallels to Mary's delivery of Christ and Christ's defeat of Satan are obvious. In Revelation, a great battle ensues in which "the dragon" and his satanic forces clash with Michael and his angels, and are overthrown and cast down "into the earth."[84] Here the dragon is to be overcome by the Christian believers themselves, by means of "the blood of the Lamb and the word of their testimony" (12:11).[85] Since the Son (Jesus) still lives eternally despite the dragon's best efforts, the dragon in a fury goes off "to make war" with the woman's other children. These other children are all believers who "keep the commandments of God, and have the testimony of Jesus Christ" (12:17).

Ironically, in the popular Roman accounts of the story of Leto and her children, the Roman emperor is usually identified symbolically with Apollo, who kills the dragon (the enemies of Rome). However, in John's vision, the place of Apollo is taken by Christ the Messiah and those who follow Him, while the terrible dragon thus represents Satan working through Rome itself and its emperors. Rome is then seen not as the conquering hero, but as the ferocious and oppressive persecutor. Further, here in Revelation, the dragon is not overcome by political and military power, but by the spiritual power of Jesus' blood and the Word of God proclaimed by the Christian believers.

A horrible beast then appears having "seven heads and ten horns, and upon his horns ten crowns, and upon his heads the names of blasphemy"

---

[84] Elsewhere in the New Testament, the defeat of Satan by means of Christian evangelism again is portrayed as a "casting down to earth." For example, when Jesus' disciples return "with joy" from their successful evangelism tours, Jesus says, "I beheld Satan as lightning fall from heaven" (Luke 10:17-18). Here in Revelation, with the aid of angelic forces, another "casting down" of Satan occurs as believers hold to "the word of their testimony."

[85] Again using the passage from Luke's Gospel in the previous footnote, in the very next verse, Jesus tells his followers, "Behold, I give you power to tread on serpents and scorpions, and over all the power of the enemy: and nothing shall by any means hurt you" (10:19). The "casting down" of the dragon and its defeat by Christian believers here in Revelation parallel the similar words spoken earlier by Jesus.

(13:1). Since this beast will re-appear in a later "snapshot" in this chapter, we will not discuss it here. A second beast appears, about which John provocatively states, "Here is wisdom. Let him that hath understanding count the number of the beast: for it is the number of a man; and his number is Six hundred threescore and six" (13:18). It is tempting at this point to dive into the ongoing controversy about the infamous number "666"; however, this temptation must be resisted, as this particular passage will be discussed extensively (and the identity of the Antichrist revealed) in the next chapter. For now, it is enough to note that all of the wondrous and spectacular images in this "snapshot" of the Seven Thunders can be explained adequately by their preterist interpretation, without recourse to futurist speculation.

Snapshot # 5: Seven Plagues (Chapters 15-17a):

"And I saw another sign in heaven, great and marvelous, seven angels having the seven last plagues. . . . And I heard a great voice out of the temple saying to the seven angels, Go your ways, and pour out the vials of the wrath of God upon the earth" (Rev. 15:1, 16:1). In the last "snapshot," we saw the image of the wonderful Mother clothed with the sun and crowned with twelve stars, she who gives birth to the Child "who was to rule all nations with a rod of iron" (12:1-5). In this snapshot of the Seven Plagues, we will encounter a very different woman indeed. This is the "Great Whore," the Harlot of Babylon who rides upon a scarlet seven-headed beast.

Again the "vials" (bowls) of plagues, as they are poured out by seven angels, are reminiscent of the plagues of Egypt: water turning to blood, darkness, hail, "frogs" which are actually deceiving spirits, and so on (Chapter 16). After these plagues are described, one of the angels then says to John, "Come hither; I will show unto thee the judgment of the great whore that sitteth upon many waters" (17:1). Because of the reference to "many waters," some have assumed this symbolic harlot to be Rome within the Italian peninsula; however, the "waters" are explained by the angel: "The waters which thou sawest, where the whore sitteth, are peoples, and multitudes, and nations, and tongues" (17:15). We see then that the reference is not to literal water at all, but to a location where many cultures and peoples converge. The angel then tells John, "The woman which thou sawest is that great city" (17:18). Again, although many think of the angel's words as applying to Rome, "that great city" has also been previously described by John when discussing the "two witnesses": "And their dead bodies shall lie in the street of *the great city* . . . where also our Lord was crucified" (11:8, emphasis added). So the harlot represents a great and multicultural city, and this great city has already been identified by John as the city of the Lord's crucifixion.

The woman is in fact a picture of Jerusalem in its apostate condition, joined in league with the Roman Empire, the seven-headed beast seen previously. For an example of Jerusalem's cosmopolitan and multicultural composition, remember that these "peoples, multitudes, nations, and tongues" were gathered together on the Day of Pentecost in Jerusalem: "Parthians, Medes, Elamites, Mesopotamians, Judeans, Cappadocians, Asians, Phrygians, Pamphilians, Egyptians, Libyans, Romans, Jews, proselytes, Cretans, Arabians," and so on (Acts 2:9-11). The traffic through Jerusalem was so general that even the plaque nailed above Jesus' head at the Crucifixion had to be written in three languages (John 19:20).

This "great city" is also described as being "divided into three parts" as it is conquered by armies crossing the Euphrates River (Rev. 16:12, 19). Again, this is explainable as a depiction of first-century Jerusalem: "While the defenders of Jerusalem split into three factions . . . the Roman armies passed easily over the Euphrates River."[86]

Is Jerusalem ever described as Babylon elsewhere? Yes; in fact, this description occurs elsewhere even in Revelation itself. In chapter 14, John sees and hears an angel proclaiming, "Babylon is fallen, is fallen, that great city" (vs. 8). A moment later John sees "a white cloud," symbolic of judgment, and upon the cloud a figure "like unto the Son of man, having on his head a golden crown" (Jesus, the Messiah) and holding a sickle. Three angels appear who encourage Christ to "thrust in his sickle into the earth"; when this happens, the resulting harvest is gathered and cast "into the great winepress of the wrath of God. And the winepress was trodden *without the city*" (vss. 14-20, emphasis added). Virtually all commentators, whether preterist, futurist, or otherwise, agree that this city is Jerusalem, the site of the judgment foreseen by John. It follows, therefore, that this city (Jerusalem) is also the "Babylon" whose fall and destruction is proclaimed by the angel.

Other commentators have also identified the Harlot of Babylon with Jerusalem; for instance, noted New Testament scholar N.T. Wright points out that in Old Testament prophecy the city of Babylon is to be judged while Jerusalem is saved, but adds that in the New Testament an ironic twist occurs: "Jerusalem has become Babylon; Jesus and his disciples have become Jerusalem. . . . Jerusalem's fall, and the disciples' flight and escape,

---

[86] Timothy Paul Jones, David Gundersen, and Benjamin Galen, *Rose Guide to End-Times Prophecy*. Torrance, California: Rose Publishing, 2011: 262.

will be the final acting out of the predictions that Babylon would fall."[87] Wright then mentions rather quietly (in a footnote) that "this conclusion may be held by some to carry implications for the reading of Revelation 17-19" regarding the identity of the harlot, and refers to another scholar who also suggests that "the great and wicked city is not Rome but Jerusalem."[88]

Another echo from the Old Testament prophets reinforces this identification. In Chapter 18 of Revelation, a different angel cries out, "Babylon the great is fallen, is fallen" (vs. 2). John continues, "I heard another voice from heaven, saying [regarding this city]. . . . She saith in her heart, I sit a queen, and am no widow, and shall see no sorrow. Therefore shall her plagues come in one day, death, and mourning, and famine; and she shall be utterly burned with fire" (18:4-8). This image clearly refers back to the previous destruction of Jerusalem witnessed by Jeremiah the prophet in 586 B.C. at the "Babylonian Captivity," for Jeremiah's lament over the city opens with the words, "How doth the city sit solitary, that was full of people! How is she become as a widow!" (Lamentations 1:1). We should note again the shifting use of imagery in Revelation: In Jeremiah's lament, Jerusalem is utterly ruined by the Babylonians themselves; the city becomes "as a widow," for it appears that the judgment of God has replaced her covenantal marriage relationship to the Lord as her husband. However, in Revelation she denies her own loss: "I sit a queen, and am no widow." The city of Jerusalem itself has become the Babylon which is predicted to fall, and does not even recognize herself as a "harlot." She has rejected her marriage to God by rejecting his appearance in Jesus Christ, but continues mistakenly to believe that her covenantal relationship to God remains secure: "I am no widow."

No wonder the angel warns, "Come out of her, my people, that ye be not partakers of her sins, and that ye receive not of her plagues" (Revelation 18:4). Believers in Christ are warned, as they had been previously warned by Christ Himself,[89] to leave Jerusalem/Babylon before its judgment takes place. Historically, this exodus out of Jerusalem actually does take place; as Eusebius records, "The whole body, however, of the church at Jerusalem, having been commanded by a divine revelation, given to men of approved piety there before the war, removed from the city, and dwelt at a certain

---

[87] N.T. Wright. *Jesus and the Victory of God: Christian Origins and the Question of God, Volume 2*. Minneapolis: Fortress Press, 1996: 356, 358.

[88] Ibid., p. 358n141. The other author to whom Wright refers is J. Massynberde Ford, in his *Revelation: Introduction, Translation, and Commentary*, part of *The Anchor Bible* series. Garden City, New York: Doubleday, 1975.

[89] In, for example, Matthew 24:15-21.

town beyond the Jordan, called Pella. Here, those that believed in Christ . . . removed from the city, as if holy men had entirely abandoned the royal city itself, and the whole land of Judea." It appears that at least the majority, if not all, of Christians in the area of Jerusalem had heeded the warnings of Christ, John, and their own prophets, and had moved away from the city before the Roman siege.[90]

But why is Jerusalem depicted as a harlot who sells her favors to the nations of the world? Actually, this depiction of Jerusalem as a prostitute, an unfaithful wife, an adulteress against God her covenantal Husband, is rather common in Hebrew prophecy, being found in several different books:

- "The land hath committed great whoredom, departing from the Lord. . . . Rejoice not, O Israel, for joy, as other people: for thou hast gone a whoring from thy God" (Hosea 1:2, 9:1)
- "Thou hast played the harlot with many lovers. . . . For all the causes whereby backsliding Israel committed adultery I had put her away, and given her a bill of divorce; yet her treacherous sister Judah [primarily Jerusalem] feared not, but went and played the harlot also" (Jeremiah 3:1, 8)
- "Thus saith the Lord unto Jerusalem. . . . Thou didst trust in thine own beauty, and played the harlot because of thy renown, and poured out thy fornications on every one that passed by [with the Egyptians, Assyrians, Chaldeans, and so on]. Wherefore, O harlot, hear the word of the Lord . . . I will gather all thy lovers . . . and I will judge thee . . . and I will give thee into their hand, and they shall throw down thine eminent place, and break down thy high places" (Ezekiel 16:3, 15-ff.)
- And so on.

Likewise we see in Revelation the seven-headed beast (the Roman Empire) turning against the harlot who sits upon it: "The beast . . . shall hate the whore, and shall make her desolate, and naked, and shall eat her flesh, and burn her with fire" (Rev. 17:16). The city of Jerusalem is literally burned with fire as it is overcome by the Romans in September, A.D. 70. One reason for this judgment from God is given: "And I saw the woman drunken with the blood of the saints, and with the blood of the martyrs of Jesus. . . . And in her was found the blood of prophets, and of saints, and of all that were slain upon the earth" (17:6, 18:24).

---

[90] *Ecclesiastical History*, Book III, Chapter 5.

This judgment of Jerusalem as the Great Whore of Babylon, responsible for the deaths of both Christian saints and Hebrew prophets, is foretold exactly both by Christ Himself and by the Apostle Paul:

From Christ: "Wherefore, behold, I send unto you prophets, and wise men, and scribes: and some of them ye shall kill and crucify; and some of them shall ye scourge in your synagogues, and persecute them from city to city: that upon you may come all the righteous blood shed upon the earth. . . . Verily I say unto you, All these things shall come upon this generation. *O Jerusalem, Jerusalem, thou that killest the prophets* and stonest them which are sent unto thee, how often would I have gathered thy children together, even as a hen gathereth her chickens under her wings, and ye would not! Behold, your house is left unto you desolate." (Matthew 23:34-38, emphasis added)

From Paul: "For ye, brethren, became followers of the churches of God which in Judea are in Christ Jesus: for ye also have suffered like things of your own countrymen, even as they have of the Jews: who both killed the Lord Jesus, *and their own prophets*, and have persecuted us; and they please not God, and are contrary to all men: forbidding us to speak to the Gentiles that they might be saved, to fill up their sins always: for the wrath is come upon them to the uttermost." (1 Thessalonians 2:14-16, emphasis added)

The harlot drunk with the blood of prophets, saints, and martyrs vividly represents the unfaithful city itself. The Harlot of Babylon is not Rome, but rather apostate Jerusalem in league with Rome, as we have seen for the following reasons:

- It is described as a "great city," and the "great city" in Revelation has previously been identified as the place "where also our Lord was crucified" (Jerusalem). The very name "Babylon" is used elsewhere in Revelation (Chapter 14) for the city of Jerusalem.

- It is described as a cosmopolitan and multicultural place; elsewhere in the New Testament we find that this description fits Jerusalem.

- The city is divided into three factions as it is attacked by armies from across the Euphrates River, all of which happened to Jerusalem during the Jewish/Roman War.

- It is described as a prostitute, which is a common description from the Hebrew prophets of Jerusalem in particular and Israel in general when turned away from God her Husband. This description could not be applied to Rome, which did not possess this covenantal relationship, like a husband and wife, with God.

- The city is described as one which persecuted and killed both the Jewish prophets and the Christian saints, which fits the description of Jerusalem given by Jesus Himself and the Apostle Paul.

- It is prophesied that the "beast" (the Roman Empire) would turn against the harlot and "burn her with fire," which is fulfilled at the destruction of Jerusalem in the year 70.

So we see once again that the better interpretation of these characters and events lies in the preterist acceptance of the bulk of Revelation as a picture of the first-century judgment against Jerusalem, not as a picture of events in John's far distant future.

Snapshots # 6 and # 7: Seven Mountains and Seven Kings (Chapters 17b-18):

In the midst of the bowls poured out as seven plagues, John describes the beast upon which the Harlot of Babylon sits: "I saw a woman sit upon a scarlet-colored beast, full of names of blasphemy, having seven heads and ten horns" (17:3); this is the same beast we have already seen in Chapter 13, with each horn having its separate royal crown (13:1). An angel explains the symbolism of the beast and especially of its seven heads: "Wherefore didst thou marvel? I will tell thee the mystery of the woman, and of the beast that carrieth her, which hath the seven heads and ten horns. . . . The seven heads are seven mountains, on which the woman sitteth. And there are seven kings: five are fallen, and one is, and the other is not yet come; and when he cometh, he must continue a short space" (17:7, 9-10). Since Rome is well known as "the city on seven hills," the "seven mountains" represent the Roman Empire in league with the harlot, the city of Jerusalem, which the beast actually hates. The seven kings are the first seven Caesars; the sixth one, Nero, is still ruling even as John writes down his vision. The seventh is Galba, who reigns only a short time (around seven months) and is quickly followed by Otho and Vitellius, numbers eight and nine of the Caesars, who also rule an even shorter time.

This time of chaos within the Roman Empire is known as "The Year of Four Emperors" because of its rapid transitions of leadership. However, after the passing of Nero, Galba, Otho, and Vitellius, a measure of order is restored when Vespasian seizes the Emperorship in December of A.D. 69; Vespasian, of course, is the general who heads the attack on Jerusalem in the Jewish/Roman War and who passes his leadership in that war to his son, Titus. Vespasian is thus both the tenth Caesar and the last of the "ten horns," since it is under his imperial leadership that Jerusalem is finally taken and destroyed. Jerusalem's destruction is the culmination of the despotism and oppression of the Roman Empire directed against Israel for well over a century, under all of the first ten Roman Caesars: "And the ten horns which thou sawest upon the beast, these shall hate the whore, and shall make her desolate and naked, and shall eat her flesh, and burn her with fire" (17:16). The ten horns, as the angel explains, are ten kings who give their "power and strength" to the beast, the Roman Empire (17:12-13); they are the Roman dictators from the first one, Julius Caesar, to the tenth, Vespasian, who actually concludes the destruction of Jerusalem.

This system of "seven cycles of seven events" concludes in Chapter 18 of Revelation with an intricate, detailed, and poetic lament over the passing of Jerusalem ("Babylon"); yet even within the lament is contained the following: "Rejoice over her, thou heaven, and ye holy apostles and prophets; for God hath avenged you on her. . . . And in her was found the blood of prophets, and of saints, and of all that were slain upon the earth" (18:20, 24).

In Summary:

Perhaps a quick summary of events could conclude our overview of the Book of Revelation and serve as a transition into the next chapter:

- Jesus comes in the clouds in judgment against those rejecting Him.
- The Jewish/Roman War forms the major part of this judgment and lasts seven years, from A.D. 66 to 73.
- Generals Vespasian and Titus lead the Fifteenth Apollonian Legion and three other legions like a swarm of horrible locusts against Jerusalem (the symbol of locusts being used because locusts are sacred to Apollo and because they can cause famine).
- Halfway through the seven-year war in the year 70, there is a five-month siege of the city, and a great starvation. The "great tribulation" follows.
- One-third of those living in and immediately around Jerusalem die.
- The city, the "Harlot of Babylon," is taken and the Temple destroyed; Jerusalem is then overrun by the Gentile forces for the remaining three and one-half years of the war.
- All of these events begin under the sixth Caesar (Nero) and conclude under the tenth (Vespasian), the "sixth head" and "tenth horn" of a terrible beast seen by John.
- However, a great multitude of Christians and believing Jews are saved.

This completes our seven "snapshots." What happens next, in Chapters 19-22 of Revelation, is a subject of dispute and discussion even among preterists, let alone between preterists and futurists. We will take up these four chapters in the pages to come.

Doubtless there are many specific details of Revelation which remain unexplained by this brief tour. However, enough has been seen for us to hold that the preterist interpretation is much more likely and accounts for much more of Revelation's overall message than the speculative and even bizarre interpretations placed upon the book by the futurist stance. We should not force Revelation into the futurist framework when a better, more likely, and more explanatory option is available: the option of Prophecy Without Panic.

12. Fifteen More Questions About Revelation

"Blessed is he that readeth, and they that hear the words of this prophecy, and keep those things which are written therein: for the time is at hand" (Revelation 1:3).

Now that we have taken a general overview of the entire Book of Revelation from the preterist perspective, it might be worthwhile to address a few more questions in the attempt to gain more specific knowledge of the figures and symbols used in the book. In particular, we should still keep in mind the questions raised earlier on: *What did the early Christians—the very first ones who read and heard the Book of Revelation—think of it?* What did they think it meant? How did they interpret it? Since we have seen that Revelation would have had great personal meaning and relevance for first-century Christians, especially those living in and around Jerusalem, those early believers must also have had certain ideas and interpretations in mind as they pondered its images, its characters, and its predicted events. What might those ideas and interpretations have been? Was there anything happening in the first-century Church that would have fit the predicted events in Revelation? Let us address these topics in a series of short questions and answers:

(1) When was Revelation written?

This may seem to be an insignificant and even odd question with which to begin; however, it has great relevance. Many biblical scholars, including all futurists, maintain that Revelation was written at the very end of John's life somewhere around A.D. 95. However, if this is true, then the preterist belief regarding one of Revelation's explicit purposes (that Revelation, in addition to its purpose of glorifying the Lord, was written as a warning to the faithful before the fall of Jerusalem in A.D. 70) would be undermined. As it happens, however, John himself does not leave us guessing, but gives us the timeline for the book. This timeline has been previously discussed, but fits in here as well because it segues nicely into the following question; therefore, allow me to repeat myself from Chapter 4:

When was Revelation written? In Chapter 17, John writes of a horrible beast with seven heads before immediately telling us that the seven heads are "seven mountains" and "seven kings." The city on seven mountains is

Rome itself; of the seven kings John writes, "Five are fallen, and one is, and the other is not yet come; and when he cometh, he must continue a short space" (17:10). The five leaders of Rome who "are fallen" are Julius Caesar, Augustus Caesar, Tiberius Caesar, Caligula Caesar, and Claudius Caesar, all of whom had already died much previously. The seventh king who rules only "a short space" is Galba Caesar, who only rules about seven months. The sixth ruler in between—the one of whom John says "one is" (in other words, is alive while John is writing)—is Nero Caesar. Nero dies in A.D. 68. Therefore, if Nero is still alive while John is writing, then John's prophecies of the soon coming of Jesus are written just before the cataclysmic events of A.D. 70, probably sometime in the mid-60s or just before Nero's death in 68. In fact, the Syriac version of Revelation from around the year 400 opens as follows: "The Revelation which was made by God to John the evangelist in the island of Patmos, into which he was thrown *by Nero Caesar*" (emphasis added). This dating, of course, fits perfectly with the preterist interpretation of these events.

There is only one bit of testimony against this dating and in favor of the later date. Eusebius quotes the church father Irenaeus as saying, "If, however, it were necessary to proclaim his name (i.e., Antichrist) openly at the present time, it would have been declared by him who saw the revelation [John], for it is not long since it was seen, but almost in our own generation, at the close of Domitian's reign."[91] Since Domitian's reign ended in A.D. 96, it appears that Irenaeus could have been speaking of John's vision being seen at the close of Domitian's reign, in the mid-90s. However, Irenaeus very well could have been speaking of John himself; the phrase "it was seen" is rather ambiguous and could be read as "he was seen." In the latter case, the words would refer to John rather than to the Revelation, since John did live well into Domitian's reign. In other words, it could mean that John was still alive and present at or near the close of Domitian's reign, not that his vision took place then. For the dating of Revelation, therefore, it seems best to go with John's own testimony in the book itself and the testimony of the Syriac version, and place its writing in the mid-60s.

(2) Who are the Antichrist and the Beast?

From the previous section, the reader may have already guessed the answers to this second question, but let us discuss it nonetheless. The relevant passage reads as follows:

---

[91] Eusebius, *Ecclesiastical History*. Book III, Chapter XVIII.

And I stood upon the sand of the sea, and saw a beast rise up out of the sea, having seven heads and ten horns, and upon his horns ten crowns, and upon his heads the names of blasphemy. . . . And I saw one of his heads as it were wounded to death; and his deadly wound was healed: and all the world wondered after the beast. . . . And it was given unto him to make war with the saints, and to overcome them: and power was given him over all kindreds, and tongues, and nations. . . . And I beheld another beast coming up out of the earth; and he had two horns like a lamb, and he spake as a dragon. And he exerciseth all the power of the first beast before him, and causeth the earth and them which dwell therein to worship the first beast, whose deadly wound was healed. . . . Here is wisdom. Let him that hath understanding count the number of the beast: for it is the number of a man; and his number is Six hundred threescore and six. (Revelation 13:1, 3, 7, 11-12, 18)

This first beast described is obviously the same creature from Chapter 17 of Revelation, as discussed in the previous chapter. The seven heads therefore are "seven mountains"; they also are "seven kings." Just as New York City is known as the Big Apple or Chicago is known as the Windy City, so Rome was known as the city on seven hills. The first beast is the Roman Empire itself; the seven heads then transmute into the first seven kings of that empire.

What about "the number of the beast" which is also "the number of a man"? The languages of Hebrew, Greek, and Latin all have a common characteristic which English does not, namely that the letters of those languages were also used to represent numbers. Consequently, words and names themselves could be represented as having the numerical values of the sum of their letters/numbers. This system is called *gematria* by Hebrew-speaking Jews and *isopsephia* by Greeks. One interesting consequence of this is that the identity of the person whose name numbers 666 *cannot be seen in English* (since English has no such numbering system), but only in the languages in common use in John's time and place. In fact, we should notice that John specifically writes that the numerical puzzle is solvable by "him that hath understanding." All of his early readers would know Greek, but for the most part only the Jews to whom his warnings were directed would know Hebrew; they would be those who would have more complete "understanding" of the puzzle.

If the puzzle of 666 is therefore solvable only in Hebrew, we should look for its Hebrew equivalents in people's names. The obvious candidate would be Nero, the Roman emperor in power at the time of John's writing, and surprisingly—or perhaps not so surprisingly—we discover that the numerical value of Nero's name does in fact line up with these scriptures. If the Greek spelling of Nero's name (*Neron Kaisar*) is transliterated into Hebrew, we get NRWN QSR; and the numerical values of these letters do add up to 666.

Another piece of compelling evidence may be adduced in favor of Nero as Revelation's Antichrist. Many Bibles specifically produced for study today have the alternate number "616" as a marginal notation to the more widely recognized 666. The reason for this is that many manuscripts survive, including some of the oldest complete copies of the New Testament, which present the number as 616 instead of 666. This marginal notation or alternate rendering seems to arise more frequently in New Testament manuscripts as they originate more closely to around A.D. 400. By that time, Latin rather than Greek had become the primary language of most of the Christian Church, and copyists and translators apparently did not want readers confused by the use of 666, even though they themselves evidently recognized that the reference was to Nero. If the Latin spelling *Nero Caesar* rather than the Greek *Neron Kaisar* is transliterated, the final N in "Neron" is dropped off, thus forming NRW QSR. The numerical values of NRW QSR add up to 616.

Other candidates for the role of Antichrist are also plausible; for example, Caligula Caesar's name adds up to 616 as well. However, only Nero's name accounts for both numbers, 666 *and* 616. Given that he also was the Emperor at the time John was writing Revelation, the weight of the evidence points toward identifying Nero as the malicious and violent 666.

On the other hand, one more point should be added. There are only four verses in the entire Bible, located in only two epistles, which specifically use the word "Antichrist."[92] All four of these verses contain certain common elements. When they refer to the Antichrist, they do not refer to one individual Antichrist; in fact, they refer to many: "Even now are there many anti-christs," as John puts it (1 John 2:18). Furthermore, they refer neither to the past (Nero) nor to the future (the futurist position of the still-to-come Antichrist); they refer to the *present*. Many antichrists, in other words, were commonly present in John's time and world, even as they are present in ours. These present-day antichrists have the characteristics of denying that Jesus is Christ (the Son of God, the Messiah) in the flesh, and they stand against the Father and against the Son, according to these four verses. Therefore, in one respect, Christians are *always* standing against the

---

[92] They are First John 2:18, 2:22, and 4:3, and Second John 7.

Antichrist; there are many people and forces contrary to the Father and to his Incarnate Son, and we hold our ground against them every day. However, this is a common feature of the Christian life throughout the ages, and it should not make us apprehensive or upset regarding the future. As always, the Greater One lives within us; the antichristian forces surrounding us are powerful, but Christ is all-powerful, and believers remain more than conquerors in Him.

(3)   What is the Harlot of Babylon?

We find the character of the Harlot of Babylon in Chapter 17 of Revelation. This woman actually represents a city, and presents a picture of Jerusalem in its apostate, unfaithful condition, joined in league with the Roman Empire, the seven-headed beast which will eventually devour her and burn her to the ground. The discussion of this answer has already been given in much greater detail in the "Snapshot # 5" section of Chapter 11, "Seven 'Snapshots' of Revelation," and the reader is referred to that discussion.

(4)   What are the Seven Years of Tribulation?

The Seven Years of Tribulation are the years of the Jewish/Roman War, from A.D 66 to 73. The tribulation period becomes the "great tribulation" halfway through this war, when Jerusalem goes through a horrible five-month siege and starvation, ending with the capture and destruction of the city and its Temple under General Titus in A.D. 70. The city is then "trodden under by the Gentiles" for the duration of the war; the Temple itself has never been rebuilt since that time.

(5)   What are the Five Months?

See the above answer; also see a more detailed discussion in the "Snapshot # 2" section of Chapter 11. In this five-month siege and famine "men shall seek death, and shall not find it; and shall desire to die, and death shall flee from them" (Rev. 9:6).

(6)   What is the 144,000?

The 144,000 is the symbolic number given for the redeemed Church, both from the Old Covenant and the New. It comes from the 12 tribes (Old Covenant) multiplied by the 12 apostles (New Covenant) multiplied by 1,000, the number of perfection and finality. They are the "first fruits" unto God from the Jewish nation of the first-century Church (Rev. 14:4), and are protected by God from the worst ravages of the time of tribulation (the war destroying Jerusalem).

We see this image also in the twenty-four elders seated around the throne of God as John's vision begins. All Christian believers, represented by the twelve tribes and the twelve apostles, "fall down" before the Lord and "cast their crowns before the throne" (Rev. 4:4, 10). For more on the

"144,000," see "Snapshot # 2: Seven Seals on a Scroll" in the previous chapter.

(7)   What are the Four Horsemen?

The "Four Horsemen of the Apocalypse," also known as "Conquest, War, Famine, and Death," ride forth as the first four Seals are opened in Revelation. They represent progressive stages in the Jewish/Roman War, including the five-month famine mentioned above. See a more detailed discussion in the "Snapshot # 2" section of Chapter 11.

(8)   What is the Abomination of Desolation?

In Matthew 24, Jesus refers to this term: "When ye therefore shall see the abomination of desolation, spoken of by Daniel the prophet, stand in the holy place . . . then let them which be in Judea flee into the mountains" (15-16). "Abomination of desolation" is best understood by comparing the parallel passage from Luke's Gospel: "And when ye shall see Jerusalem compassed with armies, then know that the desolation thereof is nigh. Then let them which are in Judea flee to the mountains" (21:20-21). Given the precise parallel language of the two prophecies, it seems obvious they are referring to the very same event. "Abomination of desolation," therefore, despite whatever else it may or may not signify, definitely refers to the time of Jerusalem being "compassed with armies," the four Roman legions surrounding the city during its siege. This is the time of Jerusalem's "desolation": "Alas, alas, that great city . . . for in one hour is she made desolate" (Rev. 18:19). For additional information, see Chapter 6, "Matthew 24 (Part 1): When Did the Whole World Hear the Gospel?"

(9)   What are Gog and Magog?

In the prophecy of Ezekiel, chapters 38 and 39, "Gog and Magog" are specifically mentioned as allying themselves with many nations rising up from "out of the north" against Israel (38:15). "Magog" means "of the land of Gog," with "Gog" evidently being a historical king; it is possible that even before Ezekiel's writings, the ancient Assyrian mention of "Gugu and Magugu" and the Greek references to "Gyges of Lydia" refer to Gog and Magog. According to Josephus, Jews of the first century identified Gog and Magog with the Scythians, living far to the north by the border of Russia; however, this identification is much disputed, with many arguing that the passage from Josephus is a much later forgery. Later Christians identified Gog and Magog as the Goths of the fifth-century Germanic uprising against the Roman Empire.

However, many of today's futurist interpreters of Revelation identify Gog and Magog with a still-future alliance between Russia (or the revived Soviet Union) and certain anti-Israel Moslem nations, most notably Turkey and Iran. Futurists base this interpretation on the prophecies in Ezekiel (with the Russian connection likely based on mistaken identification of place names mentioned by the prophet) and on Revelation 20:7-8: "And when the thousand years are expired [of the Millennium], Satan shall be loosed out of his prison, and shall go out to deceive the nations which are in the four quarters of the earth, Gog and Magog, to gather them together to battle: the number of whom is as the sand of the sea."

But if we read this passage again carefully, it seems clear that Gog and Magog are not to be identified with specific nations at all, but with all nations and peoples "in the four quarters of the earth" (not merely from the "north"). Gog and Magog, then, are all nations and peoples who stand against God and against his Christ; however, Christians are assured of their ultimate victory in Christ. The fate of these nations is related as follows: "Fire came down from God out of heaven, and devoured them. And the devil that deceived them was cast into the lake of fire and brimstone, where the beast and the false prophet are, and shall be tormented day and night for ever and ever" (20:9-10). Christ is victorious over all anti-Christian peoples and nations, even should they unite from the four quarters of the earth.

(10) Will the Temple be rebuilt in the New Jerusalem?

A staple of futurist interpretation is that the Temple will be re-built in the "New Jerusalem," and that God will once more deal with the Jews and with humans in general by means of this Temple (possibly even re-instituting animal sacrifice, in spite of the once-for-all sacrifice of Christ). For many futurist prophecy teachers, the rebuilding of a literal Temple in Jerusalem seems crucial. However, these teachers hold a certain assumption in common: that is, that the rebuilding of the Jewish Temple in Jerusalem is even *important*. My own assumption, to the contrary, is that such a rebuilding is not really very important at all. Given the vagaries of history, it may very well be the case that at some time in the future, a Jewish Temple will be rebuilt in Jerusalem on the Temple Mount currently occupied by the Islamic Dome of the Rock. But whether or not this event occurs, such a rebuilding does not actually matter all that much in God's overall salvific plan for human history. After the sacrifice of Christ, do Christians really think that we are going to go back to a system of animal sacrifice in order to try to please God? The system of Temple worship and sacrifice has been decisively rejected for the past 2,000 or so years; are we to return to that legalistic system *now*, after being the Temple of the living God through the Holy Spirit? Do Christians really believe that God wills for His Church to

98

return to the observance of the Mosaic Law for the governance of his people?

Moreover, a straightforward reading of the relevant passages in Revelation bars the futurist interpretation. In John's vision, an angel speaking to him at one point refers back to something John had heard before, a "voice of a great multitude" praising God for "the marriage of the Lamb":

> Alleluia: for the Lord God omnipotent reigneth. Let us be glad and rejoice, and give honor to him: for the marriage of the Lamb is come, and his wife hath made herself ready. And to her was granted that she should be arrayed in fine linen, clean and white: for the fine linen is the righteousness of saints. And he saith unto me, Write, Blessed are they which are called unto the marriage supper of the Lamb. (Rev. 19:6-9)

After this announcement of "the marriage of the Lamb," when John first sees the New Jerusalem, he describes it as follows: "And I John saw the holy city, new Jerusalem, coming down from God out of heaven, prepared as a bride adorned for her husband" (21:2). A few verses later, the angel approaches John and says, "Come hither, I will show thee the bride, the Lamb's wife." He then carries away John "in the spirit" to a mountain and shows John "that great city, the holy Jerusalem, descending out of heaven from God" (21:9-10). This depiction of Jerusalem as "the bride, the Lamb's wife," both great and holy, stands in stark contrast to the previous depiction of Jerusalem as the Harlot of Babylon, to be destroyed by fire. This New Jerusalem is "the bride, the Lamb's wife" and "prepared as a bride adorned for her husband"; in this vision, the great Marriage Supper of the Lamb is about to take place between Christ and his bride, the New Jerusalem.

The New Jerusalem, therefore, is plainly stated to be the Bride of Christ, which is the Christian Church. One might notice that even the white clothing of the Lamb's wife is made up of the "righteousness of saints." According to the New Testament, the Church is equally the "Bride of Christ," the "Temple of God," and the "New Jerusalem":

- "Jesus answered and said unto them, 'Destroy this temple, and in three days I will raise it up'. . . . But He spake of the temple of his body" (John 2:19-21). Note that the temple is identified with Christ's Body even during his earthly life.
- "Know ye not that ye are the temple of God? . . . . for the temple of God is holy, which temple ye are. . . . Know ye not that your body is the temple of the Holy Ghost. . . . For ye are the temple of

the living God" (1 Cor. 3:16-17; 6:19; 2 Cor. 6:16). We are both individually and collectively the temple of God.

- "Him that overcometh will I make a pillar in the temple of my God, and he shall go no more out: and I will write upon him the name of my God, and the name of the city of my God, which is New Jerusalem, which cometh down out of heaven from my God" (Rev. 3:12). Note that the overcoming believers are counted as part of the temple of God and also have the name of New Jerusalem written upon them. This image is reinforced even in more or less casual references throughout the New Testament; for example, Paul writes of "James, Cephas, and John, who *seemed to be pillars*" (Galatians 2:9, emphasis added).

- "Now therefore ye are . . . of the household of God; and are built upon the foundation of the apostles and prophets, Jesus Christ Himself being the chief corner stone; in whom all the building fitly framed together grows unto a holy temple in the Lord: in whom ye also are builded together for a habitation of God through the Spirit" (Ephesians 2:19-22). Again, the Church, not a rebuilt physical edifice, is the temple and habitation of God,

- "It is written, that Abraham had two sons, the one by a bondmaid, the other by a freewoman. . . . Which things are an allegory: for these are the two covenants. . . . For this Agar is mount Sinai in Arabia [i.e., is the covenant of the Law], and answereth to Jerusalem which now is, and is in bondage with her children. But Jerusalem which is above is free, which is the mother of us all" [i.e., all Christian believers] (Galatians 4:22-26). We see that the spiritual Jerusalem is the "mother" of the Church.

- "But ye are come unto mount Sion, and unto the city of the living God, the heavenly Jerusalem . . . to the general assembly and church of the firstborn, which are written in heaven" (Hebrews 12:22-23). Note that Christians have come to the heavenly Jerusalem *while they are still alive* here on earth.

- "I have espoused you to one husband, that I may present you as a chaste virgin to Christ" (2 Cor. 11:2). We are Christ's Bride; He is our Husband.

- "Husbands, love your wives, even as Christ also loved the church, and gave Himself for it . . . that He might present it to Himself" (Ephesians 5:25-27). Note again that the relationship of Christ to his Church is parallel to the relationship of husband and wife.

- And so on.

We see then that Paul in his epistles depicts Christians symbolically as the Bride of Christ, the Temple of God, and the "Jerusalem which is above"; John in Revelation then further spells out that identification by naming the Bride and the Temple as the "New Jerusalem," coming down from Heaven to be our eternal dwelling place. Do we therefore enter our eternal dwelling when we die? No—*that* dwelling place, our heavenly home, is a *continuation* of the eternal dwelling we enter when we become Christians and accept eternal life. **As the Bride of Christ, we are already the Temple of God and the New Jerusalem.**

So we come to the answer of the title of this section, "Will the Temple be rebuilt in the New Jerusalem?" In reply, we should by now see that the new temple of God has *already* been built in the New Jerusalem. What John sees in his vision is *the coming of the Christian Church*, the Bride of the Lamb, as God's new method of dealing with humanity. Believers themselves are the temple of the Holy Spirit (1 Cor. 6:19), and they constitute the "living stones" which are being built together as a habitation of God in the New Jerusalem, the Church of the Lord (Eph. 2:22). As the *New Living Translation* puts it, "You are living stones that God is building into his spiritual temple" (1 Peter 2:5).

Believers in Christ do not have to look forward to a physical temple in the city of Jerusalem, perhaps even with renewed animal sacrifices to deal with the sins of the human race. The sacrifice of Christ and the indwelling of the Holy Spirit are enough to establish the new Temple in the New Jerusalem, which is Christ's bride, the Church. The "Holy of Holies," which housed the presence of God in the Temple, is no longer located in a specific building or even in a specific city; it is now located in our hearts. God's eternal Presence is even now in his New Jerusalem, and will abide there eternally.

(11) What is the Millennium?

For all the fuss and debate raised through the centuries over the thousand-year reign of peace known as the Millennium, it is highly interesting that the actual word "Millennium" is never used in the Bible itself—not even once.[93] "Millennium" is derived from the Latin word for "thousand" and comes from the Latin Vulgate translation of the opening verses in Revelation chapter 20, where John writes of *annos mille* or "a thousand years":

---

[93] It is also highly interesting—and ironic—that we argue so much over exactly when the "time of peace" will begin.

101

And I saw an angel come down from heaven having the key of the bottomless pit and a great chain in his hand. And he laid hold on the dragon, that old serpent, which is the Devil, and Satan, and bound him a thousand years, and cast him into the bottomless pit [until] the thousand years should be fulfilled. . . . And I saw the souls of [believers] . . . and they lived and reigned with Christ a thousand years. But the rest of the dead lived not again until the thousand years were finished. (Revelation 20:1-5)

The controversy over the meaning of this thousand-year period matches up fairly well with the controversies over the meaning of New Testament prophecy in general.

For example, the three most common "millennial" interpretations are known as the Premillennial, the Amillennial, and the Postmillennial; the first two correspond closely to the Futurist and Preterist positions we already have been discussing. "Premillennialists," who tend also to be Rapture-oriented futurists, believe that the millennium is yet to occur in the future. Other future events such as the Rapture of the Church, the Tribulation, the Battle of Armageddon, and the Second Coming of Christ all occur before the Millennium begins (hence the "Pre" in Premillennial). Premillennialists also tend to believe that the thousand years of peace are a literal thousand years; whether or not they believe that Satan is literally "bound" with a literal "chain" during this time period is not as clearly stated. It is likely that some do and some do not.[94]

"Amillennialists," on the other hand, tend also to be some form of preterists, although some of them disagree sharply with every form of preterism, whether "partial" or "full."[95] They also tend to think of the binding of Satan as symbolic in nature: "The meaning of this binding of Satan, then, is that Christ, at His first advent, brought about a conclusive victory, leaving Satan impotent to prevent the success of God's kingdom."[96]

---

[94] The reader should notice that the arguments over whether or not we should take Revelation "literally" seem inconsistently applied. *All* readers of Revelation take some passages literally and some not; for example, I do not know of anyone who is actually waiting for a seven-headed monster to arise like Godzilla to threaten the earth. I also do not know why someone would say the "binding" of Satan with a "chain" is *not* necessarily literal, but the time period of a thousand years for this binding *is* necessarily literal. It seems more likely to me that the binding, the chain, and the thousand years are all equally symbolic.

[95] However, much of the criticism of preterism from amillennialists that I have seen makes the mistake of assuming that all preterists deny a future resurrection and final judgment—which is not the case, as I hope I have made clear.

Even though "amillennial" literally means "no millennium," most amillennialists do actually believe in the Millennium and the reign of Christ's peace. However, they believe that this reign of Christ's peace has *already begun*—in the Christian Church: "They understand the millennial kingdom to be a *present spiritual reality* while other viewpoints treat the millennium as a *future earthly event*."[97] Noted Christians who held some form of amillennialism throughout the history of the Church include Augustine, Thomas Aquinas, John Calvin, Martin Luther, and most within the Reformed and Presbyterian traditions.

It is possible that the biblical references to the thousand years of peace could refer to a literal thousand years in the future. However, I would consider it much more likely that these references concern the supernatural peace that is supposed to be currently reigning in Christ's Church: "Peace I leave with you, my peace I give unto you. . . . These things I have spoken unto you, that in me ye might have peace. In the world ye shall have tribulation: but be of good cheer; I have overcome the world" (John 14:27; 16:33). As one commentator puts it, in this view "the phrase 'thousand years' was never meant to describe a specific time span in the first place. Instead, the phrase 'thousand years' symbolizes the greatness and the glorious magnitude of the Messiah's present reign in the heavens."[98] Even though we still are facing tribulation while living in this world, we are to be of good cheer and at peace, for Christ has overcome the world and continually overcomes its power over his Kingdom.

Therefore, this period known as the Millennium may be seen as the time of Christ in his Church, a millennial reign which began in the first century; it is not necessarily something we are still awaiting in the future.

(12) What is the Parousia?

The Greek word *parousia* is used generally for an appearing, arrival, visit, or "coming." It was often used for the visit of a great leader or authority to a city, as well as that leader's entry into the city. In the New Testament, it usually bears the technical and specific meaning of "the coming of the Lord," or the Second Coming. Futurist interpreters usually take this word as referring either to the Rapture, which they see as still future, or to the Second Coming, which is to occur seven years after the Rapture and thus is also in the future. Typically, therefore, they stress that the *parousia* is "not just one event taking place at a particular time. Rather it is made up of a

[96] Steve Gregg, *Revelation: Four Views*, p. 464.
[97] Jones, Gundersen, and Galan, *Rose Guide to End-Times Prophecy*, p. 277. Emphasis in original.
[98] Ibid., p. 279.

series of events."[99] Some futurists extend this thought to refer to the Rapture and the Second Coming of Christ as the "first and second stages" of the Second Coming.

On the other hand, preterist interpreters tend to stress the idea of the *parousia* as already fulfilled: "To His Jewish judges Jesus holds out the threat of His coming even during their lifetime."[100] As stated by preterist author J. Stuart Russell, "The Parousia, or glorious coming of Christ, was declared by Himself to fall within the limits of the then existing generation."[101] In other words, the immediate and impending *parousia* of Christ prophesied by Him refers to his coming in judgment against the city of Jerusalem and the nation of Israel; this *parousia* was fulfilled in the first century. This idea of coming in judgment also is mentioned in Revelation in connection with other physical locations besides Jerusalem; for instance, Christ tells the Ephesian church, "Repent, and do the first works: or else *I will come unto thee quickly*, and will remove thy candlestick out of his place, except thou repent." He likewise tells the church of Pergamos, "Repent; or else *I will come unto thee quickly*, and will fight against them with the sword of my mouth" (2:5 and 16, emphasis added).

As we can see, then, the word *parousia* carries a somewhat ambivalent meaning. It most obviously and straightforwardly refers to Christ's coming in judgment in A.D. 70. However, it can also be taken—and I do take it in this way—as referring to a future Second Advent of the Lord, as in its use in 1 John 2:28: "And now, little children, abide in Him; that, when He shall appear, we may have confidence, and not be ashamed before Him at his Coming" [Greek *parousia*, Latin *adventu*].

In this, I am in disagreement both with futurist interpreters, who think of the "Rapture" or catching away of believers as occurring prior to the Second Coming, with both still to come in the future, and with "full" preterist interpreters, who think of the promise of the *parousia* as being completely fulfilled in the first-century judgment of Jerusalem. Rather, it seems to me that the early Christians, even after the "coming" of A.D. 70, still waited for "the Jesus who has come already" as also "the One who is

---

[99] Spiros Zodhiates, ed. *"Parousia." The Complete Word Study Dictionary: New Testament.* Chattanooga, Tennessee: AMG Publishers, 1992. Revised edition 1993. 1123-24: 1123.

[100] Oepke, Albrecht. *"Parousia." Theological Dictionary of the New Testament.* Volume V. Eds. Gerhard Kittel and Gerhard Friedrich. Grand Rapids, Michigan: Eerdmans, 1967. Reprinted 2006. 858-71: 865.

[101] Russell, *The Parousia*, p. 33.

still to come."[102] This in general reflects the position of "partial" preterism, into which camp I place myself.

Consequently, it seems best to me to accept Jerusalem's first-century destruction as the *parousia* most often predicted in New Testament prophecy, while still holding to the traditional belief in the *parousia* as expressed in the Creeds of the Christian Church: "The third day He (Christ) rose again, according to the Scriptures; and ascended into heaven, and sits on the right hand of the Father; and He shall come again, with glory, to judge the living and the dead." We may still look forward with hope to the Second Advent of the Lord, the Resurrection of the Dead, and the Final Judgment, without falling into the confused tangle of the futurist position.

By this means, partial preterists also escape the charge of holding to the "Hymenean heresy," so named from Hymeneus and Philetus in 2 Timothy 2. Paul writes of these two men, "Who concerning the truth have erred, saying that the resurrection is past already; and overthrow the faith of some" (17-18). While some preterists may hold this Hymenean position, many, including me, do not.

(13) When will the Second Coming (or Parousia) occur?

When will the Second Coming or Parousia occur? In one sense, this is the easiest question so far to answer: *No one knows*. In fact, this brings up one of the most reliable "litmus tests" of prophetic teaching: If anyone tells you he or she "knows" that the coming of the Lord is going to occur "soon," and especially if anyone names a particular time or even date for this coming (such as September 2015, the most recent date I have heard), he or she is off base.

Often prophecy teachers today have become a bit more cautious in their predictions. Instead of saying that the Parousia will occur on this or that date, they might say something like "*All the indications point to* September 2015 [or 1988, or Y2K, or 2012, etc.] as the time of the Lord's coming. All the signs in the Middle East are lining up" and so on. However, the overall effect is the same. Although these scare tactics seem to be effective in raising funds and in selling prophecy books, they are a clear sign that we should not be listening to these "headline prophets." We should rather be listening to the words of Jesus Himself:

- And He said unto them, It is not for you to know the times or the seasons, which the Father hath put in his own power (Acts 1:7).
- But of that day and hour knoweth no man, no, not the angels of heaven, but my Father only (Matthew 24:36; also Mark 13:32).

---

[102] Oepke, p. 866.

- Take ye heed, watch and pray: for ye know not when the time is (Mark 13:33).
- Be ye therefore ready also: for the Son of man cometh at an hour when ye think not (Luke 12:40).

Allow me to repeat myself: When will the Second Coming or Parousia occur? In one sense, this is the easiest question so far to answer: *No one knows*. And that is the only genuine answer I know of for that question. Anything else goes beyond the Bible.

(14) What is the Resurrection of the Dead?

Throughout the New Testament and the subsequent history of the Christian Church, one surprising fact seems to have been often overlooked or even ignored in popular Christian belief and focus: namely, that the concept of the Resurrection of the Dead is described and discussed in even greater detail than the concepts of Heaven, Hell, and the afterlife.[103] The Greek word *anastasis*, "resurrection" or "rising up," is used 42 times in the New Testament and is the primary subject of the first Christian sermon from Peter: "This Jesus hath God raised up, whereof we all are witnesses" (Acts 2:32). The Resurrection of Christ, of course, is a pre-eminent focus in the early church and into the present; in fact, Paul the Apostle stresses Christ's Resurrection so insistently in his preaching and writing that his early hearers think of him as a "setter forth of strange gods." The word "gods" is in the plural "because he preached unto them Jesus, and the resurrection" (Acts 17:18). Evidently Paul speaks so frequently of "Jesus and Anastasis," linking together Christ and Resurrection, that his auditors think he is referring to two separate deities!

Thus far so good; around the Resurrection of Christ most Christians will gather in agreement. But how are we to understand the Resurrection of the Dead in its application, not to Christ, but to believing Christians? Two options seem to present themselves in Scripture; however, this situation does not appear as an "either-or" decision, but rather as a "both-and" embrace. The first option is that believers are "resurrected" into new life when they accept salvation in Christ; the second option is that believers may still look forward in hope to the great Resurrection of the Dead at the final Parousia of Christ. Again, one is not required to choose either the first or the second option, since it seems evident that they are not contradictory; one may choose to accept both options simultaneously. As N.T. Wright

---

[103] Biblical scholar N.T. Wright discusses this surprising fact in great depth in his *Surprised by Hope: Rethinking Heaven, the Resurrection, and the Mission of the Church*. New York: HarperOne, 2008.

106

puts it, "The early Christians believed that, though the full blessings of the coming age lay still in the future, it had already begun with Jesus, particularly with his death and resurrection, and that by faith and baptism they were able to enter it already."[104] Christians live in both the present-tense deliverance out of death and into eternal life, while also hoping for and expecting the future-tense deliverance out of death by a bodily Resurrection. Furthermore, both options are directly tied to the Resurrection of Christ which we have already discussed: Christ's bodily rising brings us eternal life *today* while also serving as a guarantee of our own bodily rising *in the future*.

Jesus in John's Gospel clearly teaches the first option. He is confronted by religious critics who point out that He "said also that God was his Father, making Himself equal with God" (John 5:18). Jesus responds by making even more remarkable claims:

> For as the Father raiseth up the dead, and gives life to them; even so the Son gives life to whom He will. . . . Verily, verily, I say unto you, He that heareth my word, and believeth on Him that sent me, hath everlasting life, and shall not come into condemnation; but is passed from death unto life. (5:21, 24)

Here we see the first option, that believers are "raised up" from death and given new life by the Father and the Son, and that this "everlasting life" is attained during *this* life. When we hear the proclamation of Christ and believe on God through Him, we pass "from death unto life" and receive eternal life as a present possession. Believers are immediately and in reality "resurrected" into new life when they accept salvation in Christ. As Jesus puts it a bit later in a different situation, "He that believeth in Me, though he were dead, yet shall he live; and whosoever liveth and believeth in me shall never die." Given the startling nature of these claims, his follow-up question still seems not only pertinent, but necessary: "Believest thou this?" (John 11:25-26).

So one aspect of the Resurrection of the Dead is given here: It is a spiritual resurrection, from death unto life, which occurs *in this life* when we accept eternal life in Christ and become one of his followers. However, this does not mean that the Resurrection of the Dead is already completely over or in the past; there remains also the second aspect of this Resurrection, for believers may still look forward in hope to the great Resurrection of the Dead at the final Parousia of Christ. This grand consummation of salvation

---

[104] N.T. Wright, *Revelation for Everyone*, p. 220.

history may be seen in the concluding chapters of Revelation, after the extensive descriptions of the destruction of Jerusalem are over:

> And I saw the dead, small and great, stand before God; and the books were opened: and another book was opened, which is the book of life: and the dead were judged out of those things which were written in the books, according to their works. And the sea gave up the dead which were in it; and death and hell delivered up the dead which were in them: and they were judged every man according to their works. (Revelation 20:12-13)

This is not anything new for us at this point in our study of New Testament prophecy, as we already have seen both Jesus and Paul speak of this final trumpet, great voice, and judgment.[105] In fact, if we look back into John 5 for a moment, we find Jesus continuing his address to his critics: "The hour is coming, in the which all that are in the graves shall hear his voice, and shall come forth; they that have done good, unto the resurrection of life, and they that have done evil, unto the resurrection of damnation" (John 5:28-29). Jesus is extending even the astounding claims He has already made. Not only is He bringing eternal life to those who believe in the Father through Him in this life, but his reach encompasses even those already "in the graves." The phrase here seems too specific to be "spiritualized"; Christ is referring to the physically dead in their physical graves, who will be physically resurrected by his power for the purpose of his Final Judgment.

So what is the Resurrection of the Dead? The answer must be two-fold: It is the "resurrection" of believers into new life when they accept salvation in Christ; it is also the blessed hope of believers who look forward to the great Resurrection of the Dead at the final Parousia of Christ, a bodily rising at the last trumpet. Just as surely as the prophecies in the first part of Revelation regarding Jerusalem and Israel were fulfilled in the first century, so the prophecies in the end of the book regarding the Church and the world will also be fulfilled. They are not predictions of doom and gloom, but of joy, peace, and victory.

(15) What are the New Heavens and the New Earth?

If the reader has already come through the section on Question 14, "What Is the Resurrection of the Dead?" then he or she probably can already anticipate the similar answer to the question of this section. Like the Resurrection of the Dead, the phrase "New Heavens and the New Earth" has both a contemporary spiritual reality for the present-day believer, and

---

[105] See Chapter 9, "But Paul Writes About the Rapture, Doesn't He?"

also a more complete and final significance yet to be fully realized in our future.

In order to appreciate the phrase's contemporary spiritual significance for the present-day believer, we should start with its very first (and only) use in Hebrew prophecy. This occurs at the conclusion of the Book of Isaiah.[106] Throughout this panoramic prophecy, Isaiah primarily has been writing about Israel's conflict with the kingdom of Assyria. The Assyrians had conquered the northern kingdom of Israel and Samaria before threatening the southern kingdom of Judah. Isaiah's prophecy covers the political and spiritual background of this turbulent time, but then expands; he begins to prophesy of the coming of a Savior and Messiah, a "Righteous Servant" who would carry "the iniquity of us all" and who would "justify many; for he shall bear their iniquities" (53:6, 11). This salvation was to be offered to the Gentiles, who would be "called by a new name" (62:2). In context, this promise appears to apply to the nation of Israel; however, Isaiah then prophesies that the disobedient among the Jews would be slain by God Himself, and that God would then "call his servants by another name" (65:15).

Is this "new name" which God uses for his servants the name of "Christian"? It appears that the Apostle Paul believed so, for this specific chapter (Isaiah 65) opens with a paradoxical statement later quoted in one of Paul's epistles:

> I am sought of them that asked not for me; I am found of them that sought me not: I said, Behold me, behold me, unto a nation that was not called by my name. I have spread out my hands all the day unto a rebellious people, which walketh in a way that was not good, after their own thoughts; a people that provoketh me to anger continually to my face . . . (65:1-3)

Who is this group that "finds" the God of the Israelites even when historically not seeking for Him? Who is this "nation . . . not called by" his Name? On the other hand, who are the "rebellious people" unto whom God has repeatedly appealed despite their repeated disobedience? When the Apostle Paul quotes this passage, he makes it plain that the "disobedient and gainsaying people" (which is how he quotes Isaiah's phrase "rebellious people"[107]) is the Israel which has for the most part rejected Christ: "But to Israel he saith, All day long I have stretched forth my hands unto a

---

[106] Isaiah 65:17 and 66:22 are the only uses of this phrase in the Old Testament.

[107] Paul is quoting *apeithounta kai antilegonta*, "disobedient and gainsaying," from the Septuagint Greek rather than from the Hebrew, which accounts for the slight variation.

disobedient and gainsaying people" (Romans 10:21). The people who accept God's salvation, on the other hand, are the Gentiles, who historically had not sought the God of Abraham, Isaac, and Jacob, but who now find Him in Christ. They are those called by a new Name: the name "Christian." Previously the Bible had divided humanity into "Jews" and "Gentiles"; now, however, there is a new third grouping. Now there are Jews, Gentiles, and Christians, the "Church of God" (1 Corinthians 10:32).

What does all of this have to do with the new heavens and new earth? If we turn back to Isaiah 65, we see that these prophecies of the rise of Christianity lead directly to another, more radical way of stating the same thing:

> I will number you [those rejecting God's salvation] to the sword, and ye shall all bow down to the slaughter: because when I called, ye did not answer; when I spoke, ye did not hear; but did evil before mine eyes, and did choose that wherein I delighted not. . . . Behold, my servants [those accepting God's salvation] shall sing for joy of heart, but ye shall cry for sorrow of heart, and shall howl for vexation of spirit. And ye shall leave your name for a curse unto my chosen: for the Lord God shall slay thee, and call his servants by another name: that he who blesseth himself in the earth shall bless himself in the God of truth; and he that sweareth in the earth shall swear by the God of truth; because the former troubles are forgotten, and because they are hid from mine eyes. For, behold, *I create new heavens and a new earth*: and the former shall not be remembered, nor come into mind. (Isaiah 65:12, 14-17, emphasis added)

We for the most part do not fully appreciate the history-dividing impact of the life and teachings of Christ, along with his Crucifixion, Resurrection, and current Headship of the Church. We are surely thankful for our salvation individually; however, we must go beyond that individual thankfulness to recognize that the Church of Christ is a *supernatural* body, supernaturally created and supernaturally filled. Jesus has made a new Temple out of a new People in which God Himself now dwells by his Spirit. In other words, spiritually speaking, *we are in the new heavens and new earth right now*, which God has created through Christ. The Church is God's new way of dealing with humanity; it is God's new creation—the new creation prophesied by Isaiah and announced by Paul. The New Heavens and New Earth are a present spiritual habitation for the New Jerusalem, the Church of Christ.

However, remember that though the new heavens and new earth are a contemporary spiritual reality for the present-day believer, the prophet also envisions a more complete and final reality yet to come in our future. The prophetic vision grasps an entire universe cleansed of unrighteousness and perfected through submission to the mighty Lordship of the Savior; such a vision has surely not yet been completely fulfilled. Along this line, in his *Principles of Christian Theology*, professor John Macquarrie[108] discusses Christian eschatology (the study of "end times" and "last things") and concludes, "Eschatology has been existentially neutralized when the end gets removed to the distant future." He discusses a more "*realized* eschatology" (which in this book I have been labeling as the "full" preterist position as opposed to my own "partial" position) and remarks regarding it, "This kind of interpretation is certainly an advance on the futuristic type."[109]

Given this, it seems that Macquarrie would rest content with the idea that the new heavens and new earth are fully realized in the ongoing work of Christian salvation. However, Macquarrie does not conclude on this note, but continues:

> This kind of interpretation is certainly an advance on the futuristic type, and it has good support in some parts of the New Testament. But it is defective precisely because it gains most plausibility from being individualized, thus leaving out the whole cosmic and communal dimensions of New Testament teaching. As far as the cosmos as a whole is concerned, or even the human race, the eschatological expectations are far from being realized. . . . Only a consummating work that is coextensive with the work of creation and reconciliation can interpret the paradox of an eschatology that has already happened and that nevertheless, as it points to what has happened and is happening, holds before us the hope of what is yet to happen.[110]

Although we exist right now in God's new creation, his "new heavens and new earth" which is the current milieu of his Church, we also may look forward to the universal and all-encompassing instantiation of this New Creation in all realms everywhere, an instantiation which is, as Macquarrie

---

[108] John Macquarrie, *Principles of Christian Theology*. New York: Scribner's, 1966. Second edition, 1977. My use of Macquarrie in this passage should not be taken as implying that he would necessarily agree with my own partial preterist stance, or with my views as stated in this book. Of course, to a greater or lesser extent, the same is true of all the authors I have used or quoted.

[109] Ibid., p. 354. Emphasis in original.

[110] Ibid., pp. 354-55, 357.

puts it, "coextensive with the work of creation and reconciliation." This is the second meaning of the "New Heavens and New Earth," and, while we rejoice in the former meaning, we may likewise hope for the latter: "We, according to his promise, look for new heavens and a new earth, wherein dwelleth righteousness" (2 Peter 3:13).

Thus this promise of the new creation, while our present spiritual possession, also becomes a feature of the last things yet to come: Death for each individual; the Parousia of Christ; the Resurrection of all; the Final Judgment of all; and Eternity. All of these events are part of the traditional beliefs of the Church through the centuries; they are not to be seen as an endorsement of the Futurist prophetic position simply because they are "yet to come."

To summarize briefly:

In this chapter, "Fifteen More Questions About Revelation," we have traveled from the very beginnings of Revelation, even opening with a question as seemingly trivial as the date of Revelation's composition, all the way to a vision of the New Heavens and New Earth. Some of the questions examined definitely deal with Israel's past, while some are more amenable to applications both in the past and in the future. In fact, for now we might well remember a footnote to Jesus' extended prophecy in Mark 13 (from the *Confraternity* translation of the New Testament). This footnote states, "This long prophecy deals with both the destruction of Jerusalem and the end of the world. The elements of the prophecy are so intermingled that it is difficult at times to determine to which cataclysm Jesus refers."[111] The same could readily be said of the prophecy of the Book of Revelation as a whole: Definitely and primarily it deals with the first-century destruction of Jerusalem, yet in the concluding chapters of the book John appears also to deal with the Second Coming and Christ's final judgment of humanity, as well as humanity's eternal afterlife. The elements are so intermingled that any attempt at a definitive demarcation between them as the book concludes must of necessity be speculative.

We have seen enough, however, to assert simply and plainly that in all major (and most minor) interpretive disputes regarding the Book of Revelation, the preterist position has the better of the discussion over the futurist. Whether we list fifteen questions or fifty, the answers given by the preterist reading of Revelation just make more sense. When we ask our guiding questions of New Testament prophecy, "How does this glorify the Lord Jesus Christ?" and "How did the first Christians

---

[111] The *Confraternity* New Testament. New York: P.J. Kenedy & Sons, 1954.

understand these predictions?" a wealth of biblical illumination and spiritual reassurance floods our understanding, replacing the confusion and anxiety produced by attempting to grasp the futurist's explanations. Dispensationalist futurists seem to have their "rabbit trails" of isolated, out-of-context verses which we must learn to follow if we accept their interpretations of biblical prophecy. On the other hand, the preterist position seems to have the weight of more or less *the entire Bible* behind it. So many passages make so much more sense once we lay aside the "lens" of dispensationalism.

Furthermore, the preterist position passes what I would call the "weirdness" test. There are many futurist predictions, most in great detail, of what exactly is going to happen in the "last days." However, most of these predictions are just plain *weird*. Just for one example, in most futurist discussions of the "two witnesses" of Revelation 11, it seems that actual fire is supposed to come out of the mouths of these two witnesses, who are seen as two literal humans, and consume their enemies (11:5). If we actually believe this, it is no wonder non-Christians sometimes look at Christians as if we were lunatics! However, as we have seen, in the preterist interpretation, the fire coming out of the mouths of the witnesses is explained in the same way it is explained throughout the rest of the Bible: as the powerful and consuming Word of God which the two witnesses (the Jewish Law and Prophets) are proclaiming. This explanation makes a great deal more sense; it is the opposite of "weird."

The preterist reading, therefore, should be the one accepted by Christians and promoted to questioners rather than the overwrought speculations of the Futurist position. Correct comprehension dispels anxious apprehension—especially correct comprehension of biblical prophecy.

13. Does My View of Biblical Prophecy Really Matter All That Much?

"The stone that smote the image became a great mountain, and filled the whole earth."—Daniel 2:35

Although this book is relatively brief, the reader may feel at this point that it has been quite long enough. "Does my view of biblical prophecy really matter all that much?" you may be wondering. "Does it deserve such an extended argument? Why not adopt a 'live and let live' attitude regarding prophecy, and just let people believe whatever they want to believe?" Obviously, however, my consecutive answers to these questions will be "Yes," "Yes," and "Because ideas have real-life consequences." Differences in biblical interpretation, even in a matter as seemingly abstruse as biblical prophecy, result in different beliefs and approaches to our day-by-day Christian lives. Specifically, differences in belief bring about (1) different attitudes *toward* the Christian life, and (2) different actions *within* the Christian life.

A passage from an Old Testament prophet will help explain what I mean. The message of the Book of Daniel revolves around the Babylonian Captivity of the Jewish people, but also around the affairs of nations and empires arising after the Captivity has ended. Daniel himself issues both his own predictions and the interpretation of others' dreams regarding these historical events. For example, early on in the book, Daniel is called before the dreaded Babylonian king Nebuchadnezzar in order to interpret one of the king's dreams. This well-known dream depicts a huge statue made of various materials. Daniel describes the statue and then interprets its significance:

> Thou, O king, sawest, and behold a great image. This great image, whose brightness was excellent, stood before thee; and the form thereof was terrible. This image's head was of fine gold, his breast and his arms of silver, his belly and his thighs of brass, his legs of iron, his feet part of iron and part of clay. Thou sawest till that a stone was cut out without hands, which smote the image upon his

feet that were of iron and clay, and brake them to pieces. Then was
the iron, the clay, the brass, the silver, and the gold, broken to
pieces together and became like the chaff of the summer threshing
floors; and the wind carried them away, that no place was found
for them: and the stone that smote the image became a great
mountain, and filled the whole earth. (Daniel 2:31-35)

Daniel explains for the king the remarkable symbolism undergirding this
dream (2:36-ff.). The head of gold is King Nebuchadnezzar himself,
representing the entire Babylonian empire. Afterwards comes the next
empire, described as "silver," of lesser value than the Babylonians; this is
the Persian regime. The Persians themselves will next be replaced by the
Greeks, the empire of brass. Finally arrives the empire of "iron": not as
valuable as the others, but far stronger in military might—the Romans. At
the time of the birth of Christ, the wide-ranging Roman armies were feared
for their prowess in battle; the image of the Roman soldier is even used by
Paul for his famous "armor of God" metaphor (Ephesians 6). However,
although extremely powerful in some respects, the Roman Empire
remained weak in others, and thus the iron is "mixed" with elements of
hardened clay, easily shattered.

Something odd, however, happens in Daniel's interpretation of the
dream at this point. He describes a stone "cut out without hands"; in other
words, the origin of the stone is supernatural, not of human contrivance as
the other empires had been. During the "iron" time of the Roman Empire,
this stone appears and ultimately smashes to bits the entire system of
empires that culminates with the Roman world. According to Daniel's
interpretation, this stone then grows to become "a great mountain" and fills
"the whole earth"; later Daniel adds regarding this new supernatural
kingdom that it is "a kingdom which shall never be destroyed: and the
kingdom shall not be left to other people, but it shall break in pieces and
consume all these kingdoms, and it shall stand forever" (2:44).

When we consider all these prophetic details, there is really only one
candidate for the identity of the stone. Just as the "head of gold" represents
both Nebuchadnezzar and his empire, so the Stone represents both Jesus
Christ, "the stone which the builders rejected" (Matthew 21:42), and also
his Church, the new Kingdom in which the Lord Himself reigns. Jesus, of
supernatural origin, "cut out without hands," appears in Israel during the
days of the Roman Empire. By means of his life, death, resurrection, and
sending of the Holy Spirit, He establishes a Church which eventually brings
to an end the brutal and corrupted Roman Empire, a Church which "shall
never be destroyed" and which "shall stand forever." He is clearly the Stone

115

in Nebuchadnezzar's dream and Daniel's interpretation, and his Church is the new and everlasting Kingdom of God. So the king's dream foretells the successive overthrows of the Babylonians, the Persians, the Greeks, and the Romans, and finally the arrival of a spiritual Kingdom which shall not be overthrown.

But one other detail stands out to us as we read this account. We should note that after the coming of Jesus, the establishment of his Church, and the decline and eventual shattering of the Roman Empire, this "stone" of which Daniel writes "became a great mountain, and filled the whole earth" (2:35). Certainly, as we have seen, the Kingdom of God in his Church "shall never be destroyed" and "shall stand forever"; however, there is more to this Stone than simply its everlasting character. There is also the prophecy that Christ and his Church shall continue to grow until "the whole earth" is affected. In other words, there is more than simply the negative prophecy that the Church shall never pass away; there is also the positive prophecy that the Church shall overcome and win over the earth for the Kingdom of God.

Understanding this prophecy in this way turns the Futurist understanding on its head. The world is not necessarily to grow worse and worse, more and more committed to evildoing, until finally we are yanked out of it by the Rapture as the rest of the earth drops off into its rightful punishment. These "tired old theologies of escapism and evacuation"[112] seem so lackluster, so gloomy, so soul-deadening, compared to the *other* option presented in Daniel's prophecy, the option of hope and encouragement. This other option is that we take our stand as the Kingdom of God, growing in population as we win those around us to the Lord, until ultimately "the whole earth" becomes part of the Stone (Christianity) which becomes a Mountain, filling and infiltrating all aspects of our own lives, the lives of those around us, and the lives of our societies and cultures.

This is not to say that everyone in the world will become Christian. However, it seems that we have too quickly adopted the opposite point of view; we think that too *few* will become Christian. We have too quickly "written off" the world as destined for judgment and perdition. We speak of higher education, the arts, journalism, television, music, Hollywood, culture in general, and the vast majority of people around us as if they were irretrievable and unsalvageable. This should not be the perspective of the Mountain that fills the whole earth!

---

[112] Rob Bell. Promotional recommendation from the back cover of N.T. Wright's *Surprised by Hope: Rethinking Heaven, the Resurrection, and the Mission of the Church*. New York: HarperOne, 2008.

These details of Daniel's prophecy fold together seamlessly with some of the later teachings of Jesus. Back in Chapter 4 of this book,[113] I argued for this statement: "The preterist interpretation helps make us aware of what the Church is supposed to be doing right now." That particular section of Chapter 4 may be seen as a "preview" of what we are here discussing. For instance, I brought up an entire series of parables of Jesus with roughly the same point, from Matthew 13. Here, to illustrate this point, is the parable of the woman and the leaven:

> Another parable spake he unto them; The kingdom of heaven is
> like unto leaven, which a woman took, and hid in three measures of
> meal, till the whole was leavened. (Matthew 13:33)

As was previously discussed, the "kingdom of heaven" in Matthew's Gospel is spoken of as the "kingdom of God" in the others; there is really no difference between the two phrases except that Matthew uses the one to avoid offending his Jewish readers by the constant use of the name of God. Therefore, if we substitute the phrase "Kingdom of God" for the other, Jesus says here that the Kingdom of God, which is "among us," is like leaven transforming everything around it until all its surroundings are touched by its expansive influence and changed for the better. Although leaven is occasionally used elsewhere in the Bible to represent evil and corruption, the leaven does not represent evil here; it represents *teaching*, the presentation of the Word of God to the surrounding world. As Jesus tells his disciples at another time, "leaven" represents "doctrine" (Matthew 16:6-12). In that specific case, the leaven is the corrupt doctrine of the Pharisees; in this case of the parable under discussion, the leaven is the doctrine of the Kingdom of God; but the important point is that in both cases the use of the word "leaven" shows the influence of *teaching*, not of *evil*. Teaching can be evil, but teaching can also be helpful, positive, and life-transforming; as Jesus says, "The kingdom of heaven is like unto leaven."

Ideas have real-life consequences. Differences in how one interprets Jesus' parables lead to different attitudes toward the Christian life and our place in the world; they also lead to different actions *within* the Christian life. Nowhere are these principles more clearly seen than in one's response to these words of Christ. Futurists seem to be waiting to be snatched out by God *from* the world (by the Rapture), while preterists are working with God *to change* the world (by the Gospel). Since preterists are not bunkered down hoping for rescue, they are looking to the Lord as their ongoing source of help, not as their soon-to-appear avenue of escape. In the futurist view, no

---

[113] Chapter 4, "Why Should We Prefer the Preterist View?"

matter how evil and error-filled the world becomes, that is just fine; after the Rapture, the world will get everything it deserves in God's fiery judgment. On the other hand, in the preterist view, no matter how evil and error-filled the world becomes, there is still hope; once the Church actually accepts its mission of being the leaven mixed by God into the loaf, actively out to transform the world around us by the message of God's saving Word, we can help to change the evil and error in the world through the power of Christ.

Furthermore, the futurist looks forward to a sweeping and dramatic and sudden instantiation of the Kingdom of God, while the preterist takes these parabolic pictures as Jesus presented them: as leaven, for example, patiently and quietly and confidently working underground, behind the scenes, hidden in the loaf, until the whole is changed by the power of the Gospel. The Kingdom arrives steadily and gradually, "first the blade, then the ear, then the full corn in the ear," according to Jesus (Mark 4:26-28). This is the sort of "leavening" we as Christ's Body are to be accomplishing day by day, action by action, word by word, infusing the life of the Good News into a world damaged, deadened, and destroyed by the effects of sin. We are not hoping for our own evacuation and the world's demise, but rather for the world's very life and salvation as we remain within it and work toward its transformation.

"But," one might respond, "don't you know that only a few will be saved out of the world? Do you not recall Jesus' words, 'Strait is the gate, and narrow is the way, which leadeth unto life, and few there be that find it'? Your view of the action of the Church in the world is overly optimistic and unrealistic." Yes, Jesus did teach this—in fact, He taught it on more than one occasion. These quoted words appear in the Sermon on the Mount (Matthew 7:14), but also in a parallel passage in Luke's Gospel in which a disciple asks directly, "Lord, are there few that be saved?" In this parallel passage, immediately after Jesus repeats this saying ("Strive to enter in at the strait gate: for many, I say unto you, will seek to enter in, and shall not be able"), He explains Himself as follows.

When the "Master of the house" shuts his door, some will "stand without" and knock, saying, "Lord, Lord, open unto us." When the Master responds, "I know you not" and "Depart from me," these who are unable to enter will explain who they are: "We have eaten and drunk in thy presence, and thou hast taught in our streets." But the Master will again say, "Depart from me, all ye workers of iniquity" (Luke 13:23-27). Jesus then concludes:

There shall be weeping and gnashing of teeth, when ye shall see Abraham, and Isaac, and Jacob, and all the prophets, in the kingdom of God, and you yourselves thrust out. And they shall come from the east, and from the west, and from the north, and from the south, and shall sit down in the kingdom of God. And behold, there are last which shall be first, and first which shall be last. (Luke 13:28-30)

Who are these knocking on the Master's door but not able to enter? In their very own words, they identify themselves, for they tell the Master that they have "eaten and drunk" in his presence, and even that He has taught in their very own streets. These of whom Jesus is speaking are the first-century Jews who for the most part rejected Him and his message; of those first-century Jews, only a relative few "entered in" at God's invitation and were saved. The majority continued their own ways onward, concluding in that generation at the judgment of God in A.D. 70.

In context, we are able to recognize that Jesus is *not* saying that only a few will become Christians and be saved; in fact, we should have been able to recognize this simply from the subsequent history of the growth of the Christian Church. To the contrary, Jesus prophesies that people shall enter the Kingdom of God "from the east, and from the west, and from the north, and from the south." This predicts the inrush, the flood, of converts from the non-Jewish world; these converts would sit with Abraham, Isaac, and Jacob in the Kingdom of God, while those who trusted in their Abrahamic identity rather than partaking of Abraham's faith would be excluded. Those thinking of themselves as "first" and others as "last" solely because of their previous heritage and ethnicity suddenly find their positions reversed in God's judgment. This view is neither "overly optimistic" nor "unrealistic"; to be sure, it is optimistic regarding the salvation of many, but it is realistic as well. Not all will be saved.

But can we not pray, as Jesus indicates, that massive numbers and whole peoples and entire nations from out of the world turn to Christ and be saved? "I exhort therefore," writes Paul, "that, first of all . . . prayers, intercessions, and giving of thanks, be made for all men. . . . For this is good and acceptable in the sight of God our Savior; who will have all men to be saved, and to come unto the knowledge of the truth" (1 Timothy 2:1-4). In fact, should we not continue to pray for the Jewish people as well? "For the grace of God that bringeth salvation hath appeared to all men" (Titus 2:11). Should we not pray for and work toward the salvation of the world—that the "east, west, north, and south" come into the Kingdom of

119

God? Contrary to the "end-times" preconceptions of some, *the loss of the majority of the world does not seem inevitable.*

We can see, therefore, that our interpretation of biblical prophecy is neither trivial nor merely academic. In fact, a great deal of our Christian attitudes and actions depends on it.

§

How shall we wrap up and summarize this discussion and even this entire book? In the final week of his earthly life, Jesus gives a parable pronouncing God's judgment upon those rejecting Him, which may well serve as our summary and conclusion. Allow me to quote it, adding explanatory material in brackets and highlighting two relevant points in particular:

> And Jesus answered and spake unto them again by parables, saying, The kingdom of heaven is like unto a certain king [God the Father], which made a marriage for his son [Christ], and sent forth his servants [the prophets] to call them that were bidden to the wedding [the nation of Israel as a whole]: and they would not come. Again, he sent forth other servants [the Lord's apostles], saying, Tell them which are bidden: Behold, I have prepared my dinner: my oxen and my fatlings are killed, and all things are ready: come unto the marriage [the salvation prepared through Christ]. But they made light of it, and went their ways, one to his farm, another to his merchandise: and the remnant took his servants, and entreated them spitefully, and slew them [the persecution of the prophets and early Christians]. But when the king heard thereof, he was wroth: and he sent forth his armies [the Gentile forces used as God's instruments of judgment], and destroyed those murderers, and *burned up their city.* Then saith he to his servants, The wedding is ready, but they which were bidden were not worthy. *Go ye therefore into the highways, and as many as ye shall find, bid to the marriage.* (Matthew 22:1-9, emphasis added)

Here the specific judgment foretold by the Lord comes to pass: Jerusalem itself was to be destroyed, being "burned up" with fire, and the marriage or salvation of God's Son was to be offered to non-Jews. As Jesus points out elsewhere, He was "not sent but unto the lost sheep of the house of Israel"; however, even the non-Jews eagerly "eat of the crumbs" of salvation once the Messiah has been rejected (Matthew 15:24-27). The Apostle Paul explains this further in his letter to the Romans: The "gospel of Christ" is "the power of God unto salvation to everyone that believeth; to the Jew first, and also to the Greek [the non-Jewish world]" (Romans 1:16). God's great plan of salvation through Christ, offered first to Israel, has not abandoned the Jews entirely, but has now been *expanded* to include the rest of humanity as well. This is the main point and best understanding of the majority of New Testament prophecy.

So the Messiah is rejected, Jerusalem destroyed by burning, and the Jewish people scattered into the "Diaspora" world. But there is yet a second highlighted sentence which we should examine. What about those accepting the salvation of the Lord, those believing in the message of Christ? The King in the parable has specific instructions for them as well; He tells his servants, *"Go ye therefore into the highways, and as many as ye shall find, bid to the marriage."*

This is our job now. This is what the Christian Church should be doing: not watching the world decay into a morass of ignorance, biblical misunderstanding, ethical relativism, and blind pursuit of unsatisfactory pleasures; not complacently sinking into irrelevance as we passively await our own "escape" via the "Rapture" from the problems of fellow humans; not responding with pettiness and vindictiveness as we observe the worsening plight of those around us, thinking, "Well, that's what they deserve; they should have accepted the Lord back when the Church had the courage and compassion actually to *talk* to those around it." No, we should be infiltrating all areas of the world, like God's spies, like undercover agents of faith, holding out in all things the Way, Truth, and Life. On our jobs, in our classrooms, in our families, with our friends, in our marriages, in the media, in politics, in the armed services, in our recreational activities, wherever we may be, as much as we can with the Lord's help—should we not shine like beautiful stars in the Kingdom of God for those with eyes to see? As many as we encounter, as many as we find, we must bid to the Marriage; we must hold forth the wondrous redemption of our loving Father and his faithful Son, with the powerful Holy Spirit motivating and empowering us in our witness. Even if this is, as some claim, a "post-Christian" society, in God's power *there is always hope. What is post-Christian can become Christian again.* As ambassadors of Christ, let us become the leaven transforming the loaf; let us not wait to be "rescued" *from* the world, but rather become the rescuers *of* the world. This is our calling; this is our joy and fulfillment; this is our Lord loving and ministering through us even as He did in his own earthly life.

Pastors, publishers, ministers, media producers, and readers inclusively, I plead with you in the name of a fruit of the Spirit (peace) and in the name of a gift of the Spirit (knowledge): It is well past time for the futurist explanations of biblical prophecy to be moved aside. It is perhaps even time for the Church as a whole to issue a few apologies for the role these futurist explanations have played in fostering an atmosphere of anxiety and apprehension, an atmosphere which inevitably changes to one of disillusionment and skepticism as the foretold Raptures repeatedly fail to occur.

It is well past time for balanced and responsible teaching on biblical prophecy to become the norm and not the exception. It is well past time for the futurist stance to be shelved—and I do not mean shelved in bookstores. It is well past time that we drop completely the "tired old theologies of escapism and evacuation." It is well past time that we minister both to fellow Christians and to the world at large the understanding of Prophecy Without Panic.

Works Cited

Bibles used:

The *Confraternity* New Testament. New York: P.J. Kenedy & Sons, 1954.
The Ignatius Catholic Study Bible, 2nd edition. Revised Standard Version. San Francisco: Ignatius Press, 2010.
The Jerusalem Bible. New York: Doubleday, 1966.
King James Version. Public domain.
The Living Bible. Paraphrased by Kenneth Taylor. Carol Stream, Illinois: Tyndale House Publishers, 1974.
The New Living Translation. Carol Stream, Illinois: Tyndale House Publishers, 2006.
New Scofield Reference Bible. New York: Oxford University Press, 1967.
The New Testament: An Expanded Translation. Kenneth Wuest, trans. Grand Rapids, Michigan: Eerdmans Publishing, 1961.

Other works used:

Allison, Jr., D.C. "Eschatology." *Dictionary of Jesus and the Gospels*. Edited by J.B. Green, S. McKnight, and I.H. Marshall. Downers Grove, Illinois: InterVarsity Press, 1992.
Beale, G.K., and Sean M. McDonough. "Revelation." *Commentary on the New Testament Use of the Old Testament*. G.K. Beale and D.A. Carson, eds. Grand Rapids, Michigan: Baker Academic, 2007: 1081-1161.
Bell, Rob. Promotional recommendation from the back cover of N.T. Wright's *Surprised by Hope: Rethinking Heaven, the Resurrection, and the Mission of the Church*. New York: HarperOne, 2008.
Boyer, Paul. *When Time Shall Be No More: Prophecy Belief in Modern American Culture*. Cambridge: Belknap Press of Harvard University Press, 1992.
Bruce, F.F. "Eschatology." *The Evangelical Dictionary of Theology*. Edited by Walter A. Elwell. Grand Rapids, Michigan: Baker Books, 1984.

----. *The Hard Sayings of Jesus*. From *Hard Sayings of the Bible*. W.C. Kaiser, Jr.; P.H. Davids; F.F. Bruce; and M.T. Brauch. Downers Grove, Illinois: InterVarsity Press, 1996.

Capps, Charles. *End-Time Events: Journey to the End of the Age*. Tulsa: Harrison House, 1997.

Chesterton, G.K. *Orthodoxy* [1908]. From *Heretics/Orthodoxy* in the *Nelson's Royal Classics* series. Nashville: Thomas Nelson, 2000.

Clarke, Adam. *Commentary on Matthew*. In *Parallel Classic Commentary on the New Testament*. Edited by Mark Water. Chattanooga, Tennessee: AMG Publishers, 2004.

"Cloud." *Dictionary of Biblical Imagery*. Edited by L. Ryken, J.C. Wilhoit, and T. Longman III. Downers Grove, Illinois: InterVarsity Press, 1998.

Clouse, Robert G. "Foreword." In Steve Gregg, *Revelation: Four Views*. Nashville: Thomas Nelson, 1997.

Currie, David B. *Rapture: The End-Times Error That Leaves the Bible Behind*. Manchester, New Hampshire: Sophia Institute Press, 2003.

Draper, John. "*Left Behind* Co-Author Slams Contrary New Series." christian-retailing.com.

"End Times." *Dictionary of Biblical Imagery*. Edited by L. Ryken, J.C. Wilhoit, and T. Longman III. Downers Grove, Illinois: IVP Press, 1998.

Eusebius Pamphilus. *Ecclesiastical History*. Grand Rapids, Michigan: Baker Book House, reprinted 1993.

"Field Guide to the Wild World of Religion." Isitso.org.

Gates, David. "The Pop Prophets." *Newsweek* 24 May 2004: 46-47.

Gentry, Kenneth. *Before Jerusalem Fell*. Tyler, Texas: Institute for Christian Economics, 1989.

Gregg, Steve. *Revelation: Four Views*. Nashville: Thomas Nelson, 1997.

Hahn, Scott, and Curtis Mitch. "End of the World?" *The Ignatius Catholic Study Bible*, 2nd edition. Revised Standard Version. San Francisco: Ignatius Press, 2010: 50.

Hanegraaff, Hank. *The Apocalypse Code*. Nashville: Thomas Nelson, 2007.

Ice, Thomas. "The Myth of the Origin of Pretribulationism." pre-trib.org.

Jewett, Robert. *Jesus Against the Rapture: Seven Unexpected Prophecies*. Philadelphia: Westminster Press, 1979.

Jones, Timothy Paul, David Gundersen, and Benjamin Galen. *Rose Guide to End-Times Prophecy*. Torrance, California: Rose Publishing, 2011.

Josephus. *The Jewish War*. New York: Penguin. Revised edition, 1984.

King, Max. *The Cross and the Parousia of Christ*. Warren, Ohio: Parkman Road Church of Christ, 1986.

Koester, Craig R. *The Apocalypse: Controversies and Meaning in Western History.* Chantilly, Virginia: The Teaching Company, 2011.

Kreeft, Peter, and Ronald K. Tacelli. *Handbook of Christian Apologetics.* Downers Grove, Illinois: InterVarsity Press, 1994.

Ladd, George Eldon. "The Historic Hope of the Church." From *The Blessed Hope.* Grand Rapids, Michigan: Eerdman's, 1980. Groups.msn.com /ChristianEndTimeViews.

Lewis, C.S. "The World's Last Night." From *The World's Last Night and Other Essays.* New York: Harcourt Brace Jovanovich, reprinted 1960: 93-113.

Lindsey, Hal. *The 1980s: Countdown to Armageddon.* New York: Bantam Books, 1980.

Macquarrie, John. *Principles of Christian Theology.* New York: Scribner's, 1966. Second edition, 1977.

Martin, Dr. Walter. *Essential Christianity: A Handbook of Basic Christian Doctrines.* Revised edition. Ventura, California: Regal Books, 1980.

Massynberde Ford, J. *Revelation: Introduction, Translation, and Commentary.* From *The Anchor Bible* series. Garden City, New York: Doubleday, 1975.

Moffatt, James. "The First and Second Epistles of Paul the Apostle to the Thessalonians." *The Expositor's Greek Testament, Vol. IV.* Ed. by W. Robertson Nicoll. Grand Rapids, Michigan: Eerdmans Publishing. Reprinted 1990.

Norman, Larry. "I Wish We'd All Been Ready" (song). From the album *Only Visiting This Planet.* Solid Rock Productions, 1969.

Oepke, Albrecht. *"Parousia." Theological Dictionary of the New Testament.* Volume V. Eds. Gerhard Kittel and Gerhard Friedrich. Grand Rapids, Michigan: Eerdmans, 1967. Reprinted 2006: 858-71.

Pieters, Albertus. *The Lamb, the Woman, and the Dragon.* Grand Rapids, Michigan: Zondervan, 1937.

"Rapture teasing fueled shooter, victim's mom says." Associated Press, May 2011.

Rhodes, Ron. *Five-Minute Apologetics for Today.* Eugene, Oregon: Harvest House, 2010.

Riddlebarger, Kim. *A Case for Amillennialism: Understanding the End Times.* Grand Rapids, Michigan, and Leicester, England: Baker Books and Inter-Varsity Press, 2003.

Russell, J. Stuart. *The Parousia: The New Testament Doctrine of Our Lord's Second Coming.* Grand Rapids, Michigan: Baker Books. Reprinted 1999.

Sharps, Matthew J.; Schuyler W. Liao; and Megan R. Herrera. "Remembrance of Apocalypse Past: The Psychology of True Believers When Nothing Happens." *Skeptical Inquirer* 38.6 (Nov./Dec. 2014): 54-58.

Smith, Larry T. *The Coming of the Lord, the Last Days, and the End of the World.* Rightly Dividing the Word, 2000.

Sproul, R.C. *The Last Days According to Jesus.* Grand Rapids, Michigan: Baker Book House, 1998.

Strong, James. *Strong's Exhaustive Concordance of the Bible.* 34th printing. Nashville: Abingdon Press, 1976.

---. *Strong's Expanded Dictionary of Bible Words.* Adapted by Robert P. Kendall. Nashville: Thomas Nelson Publishers, 2001.

Thigpen, Paul. *The Rapture Trap.* West Chester, Penn.: Ascension Press, 2001.

VanderLugt, Herbert. *Perhaps Today! The Rapture of the Church.* Grand Rapids, Michigan: Radio Bible Class, 1984.

Vincent, Marvin R. *Word Studies in the New Testament. Volume I.* Originally published 1886. Peabody, Massachusetts: Hendrickson Publishers, reprinted 1985.

Vine, W.E. *Vine's Expository Dictionary of New Testament Words.* Originally published 1939. Iowa Falls, Iowa: Riverside Book and Bible House, reprinted 1952.

Walvoord, John F. *The Revelation of Jesus Christ: A Commentary.* Chicago: Moody Press, 1966.

Wright, N.T. *Jesus and the Victory of God: Christian Origins and the Question of God, Volume 2.* Minneapolis: Fortress Press, 1996.

---. *Revelation for Everyone.* Louisville, Kentucky: Westminster John Knox Press, 2011.

---. *Surprised by Hope: Rethinking Heaven, the Resurrection, and the Mission of the Church.* New York: HarperOne, 2008.

Zodhiates, Spiros, ed. *"Parousia." The Complete Word Study Dictionary: New Testament.* Chattanooga, Tennessee: AMG Publishers, 1992. Revised edition, 1993: 1123-24.

CPSIA information can be obtained
at www.ICGtesting.com
Printed in the USA
LVOW12s0801310517
536425LV00020B/612/P